Hands-On Thinking Activities

Centers through the Year

Vanessa Bredthauer

Table of Contents

Congratulations on your purchase of some of the finest teaching materials in the world.
For information about other Evan-Moor educational products,
call toll-free 1-800-777-4362 and receive a free catalog.

Entire contents copyright ©1995 by EVAN-MOOR CORP.
18 Lower Ragsdale Drive, Monterey, CA 93940-5746

Author: Vanessa Bredthauer
Illustrator: Gary Shipman
Editor: Jo Ellen Moore
Cover: Cheryl Kashata

How and Why

A frustration with seasonal classroom "parties" led me to develop this series of centers for seasonal celebrations based upon math and science activities. Students explore thinking skills in a fun-filled, hands-on way.

The centers can be set up in different ways:

- As a "carnival" where students spend two to four hours on one day traveling through the centers. This gives the day a special feeling and formally salutes the season. Students who have religious restrictions can choose to work only at those centers which don't conflict with their beliefs.

- As a series of centers done over a period of time during the appropriate season. You can set up only one or several of the centers for a specific number of days. Organize a schedule for students to follow. Change the center as the need arises.

The focus of these centers is both scientific and mathematical process skills. The individual skills being practiced are listed on the introductory page for each season and on the teacher direction page for the specific center. Students will be practicing the following skills:

- following directions
- predicting
- estimating
- interpreting
- sorting
- classifying
- organizing
- designing

In addition, children experience working independently or with a partner as they follow written directions. The hands-on approach in a non-threatening environment helps to build confidence, willingness to be a risk-taker, and self-esteem.

Helpful Hints....

If you choose the "seasonal carnival" approach:

- Prepare materials for the centers in advance.
- Call in parent and other volunteer help for the day.
- Make a booklet for each student containing all of their center information and record sheets.
- Make sure students have worked on the math or science skill being presented in the center. This should not be the first time a child sees a concept.
- Before students begin, take a "tour" of each station, walking students through what will be expected. Have them go through their student booklets at the same time.
- Traveling Rules: Students can't move to a new center until there is an empty seat at that center. If you feel your students can't handle such an unstructured method of movement, set a timer to indicate when students can move to a new center.
- Encourage students to help one another at a center before asking for adult help.

If you choose the independent center approach:

- Prepare materials for centers in advance. Choose centers that will not conflict with any religious beliefs of your students.
- Make student booklets containing only the materials needed for the centers you plan to set up.
- Make sure to review each center befor you let students work with it.
- Let at least two students work at each center. They can provide help for each other, minimizing the need for teacher help.

Follow-Up

Whichever way you decide to do the centers, be sure to build in time for closure once the centers are completed. This is an integral part of the experience.
Comparing results brings out additional points of view, new strategies and reinforces the fact that there can be more than one right answer.

Be Prepared

Have an extra activity available for students who finish early. The *seasonal categories sheet* at the beginning of each section can be used for this purpose. Include this sheet in the student booklets.

Critical Thinking Skills

This book offers teachers the opportunity to provide practice
with the following critical thinking skills:

Following Directions - putting written or oral instructions
into appropriate and productive action

Predicting - identifying a pattern and extending it to a
logical next step

Estimating - mentally approximating an answer before
or instead of doing a calculation

Interpreting - determining the sense and significance
of information or data

Sorting - putting items into groups according to a
shared attribute

Classifying - developing and labeling groups that have
consistent sets of attributes

Organizing - arranging classified groups to show
relationships between them

Designing - reorganizing already existing ideas or
information into something new

Autumn Activities

	Following Directions	Predicting	Estimating	Interpreting	Sorting	Classifying	Organizing	Designing
The Falling Leaves					🌰	🌰		
Sensible Squash				🌰			🌰	🌰
Petite Pumpkins		🌰	🌰					
The Nut Cache	🌰							🌰
Candy Counter					🌰		🌰	
Jack-o'-lantern Jamboree	🌰							🌰
Sweet Tooth Jar	🌰		🌰					
Drop by Drop		🌰		🌰				
Peter Piper's Pumpkins, foll	🌰				🌰			
Bubble Magic	🌰	🌰						

Hands-On Thinking Activities

Note: Provide this reproducible for any students who finish a center early.
* Star boxes are worth 5 points, other boxes count for 1 point. How many points can you get?

Name It	an adjective	a part of your body	something you can wear	a city, state, or country	a real or imaginary animal
EXAMPLE:**E**	excited	elbow	earmuffs	England	elk
A			*		
U		*			*
T					
U		*	*		*
M					
N					

Thinking Skills *- sorting, classifying*
Number of students at this center *- up to 4*
Time required at center *- 25 minutes*

Student Task

Students sort leaves by attributes using a Venn diagram.

Materials

- sets of leaf patterns on page 10
- envelopes
- sheets of 12" x 18" (30.5 x 45.7 cm) construction paper
- copies of the student record sheet on page 9
- center sign on page 11

Teacher Notes

1. Make a Venn diagram on each sheet of large construction paper. The diagram should fill the sheet. Laminate them if possible. These serve as work stations for the students.

2. Make four sets of leaf patterns. Color as directed on the pattern. Cut the cards apart and place one complete set in each envelope.

3. Be sure your students understand the term *attributes* (a certain quality or characteristic of an object, such as color, shape, size, smell, taste, texture, etc.) and how a Venn diagram works before they begin the activity.

4. Children will choose **two** attributes by which to sort the leaves. (Note: red leaves and yellow leaves would be only one attribute - color). They will place the leaves having one attribute in one Venn circle; and leaves with both attributes in the overlapping section of the Venn Diagram. For example:

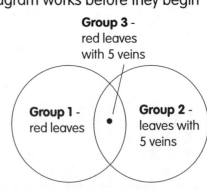

5. Students are to repeat this activity three times and record the results.

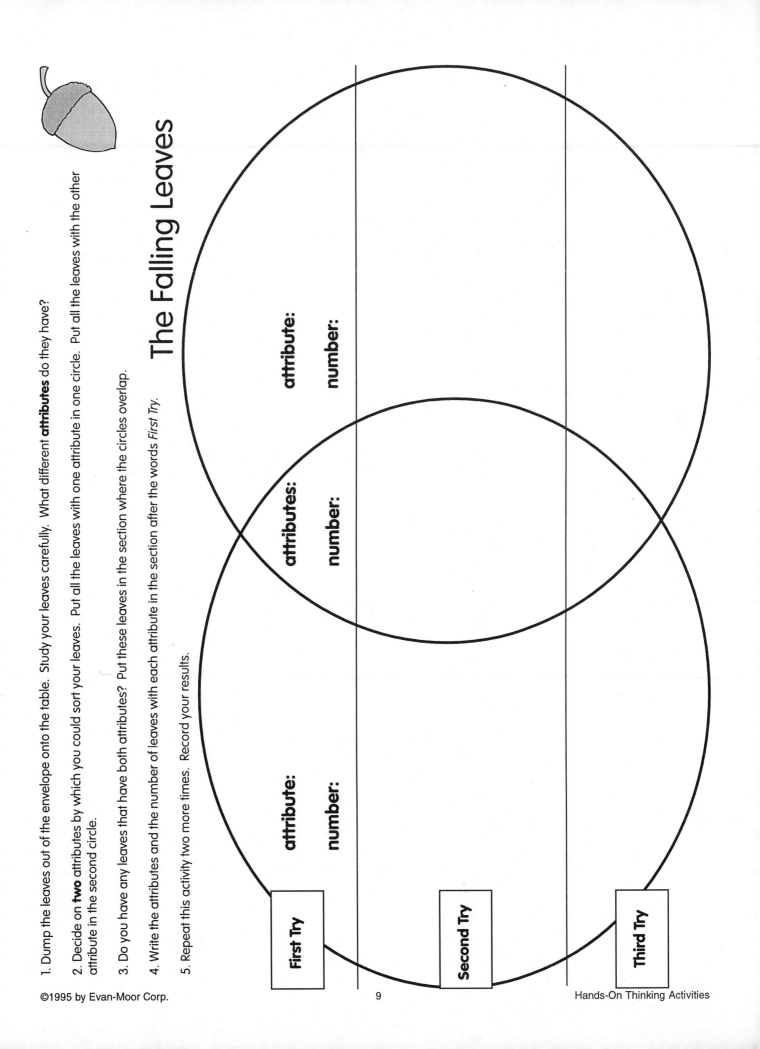

The Falling Leaves

1. Dump the leaves out of the envelope onto the table. Study your leaves carefully. What different **attributes** do they have?

2. Decide on **two** attributes by which you could sort your leaves. Put all the leaves with one attribute in one circle. Put all the leaves with the other attribute in the second circle.

3. Do you have any leaves that have both attributes? Put these leaves in the section where the circles overlap.

4. Write the attributes and the number of leaves with each attribute in the section after the words *First Try*.

5. Repeat this activity two more times. Record your results.

attribute:

number:

attributes:

number:

attribute:

number:

First Try

Second Try

Third Try

Hands-On Thinking Activities

orange   red   yellow   brown

10

Hands-On Thinking Activities

Note: Reproduce this sign to place on the table to identify each center.

fold

The
Falling Leaves

Thinking Skills - *interpreting, organizing, designing*
Number of students at this center - *up to 4*
Time required at center - *25 minutes*

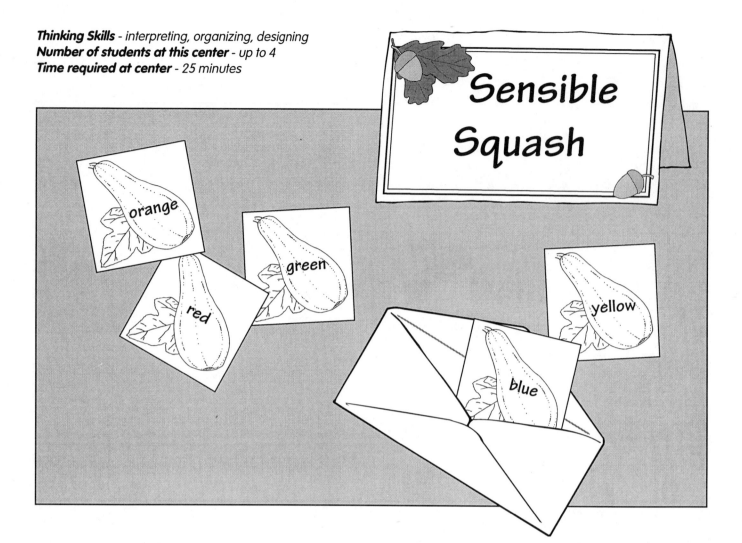

Student Task

Students follow a series of clues to find the color pattern in which the squash grew.

Materials

- sets of colored squash cards on page 14 (sets contain one each of red, green, blue, yellow, pink, and orange)
- envelopes for storing the paper squash
- small plastic bags (containing one crayon of each color: red, yellow, blue, green, pink, and orange)
- copies of the student record sheet on page 13
- center sign on page 15

Teacher Notes

1. Cut out and color the squash drawings on page 14. Paste them on stiff cardboard and laminate them. Place each set in an envelope. Encourage students to replace the squash cards in the envelope when they have completed this activity.

2. Encourage students to create more squash patterns and write the clues on the back of their record sheets.

 Hands-On Thinking Activities

Sensible Squash

This unusual plant has six squash growing on its vine. They are all different colors. Use your paper squash and the clues below to figure out the order in which they grew. When you've found the pattern, color the squash vine below to show your answer.

1. The pink squash grew to the right of the yellow squash.
2. The blue squash was found between the green squash and the yellow squash.
3. The red was the first squash on the left.
4. The orange squash was the third squash to the right of the blue squash.

Now, mix up your squash and arrange them in a secret pattern. Try writing clues that will help another student to solve your squash pattern. If you need more than four clues, write the extras on the back. Once you've written down your clues, ask other students to come and try their luck!

1. _____

2. _____

3. _____

4. _____

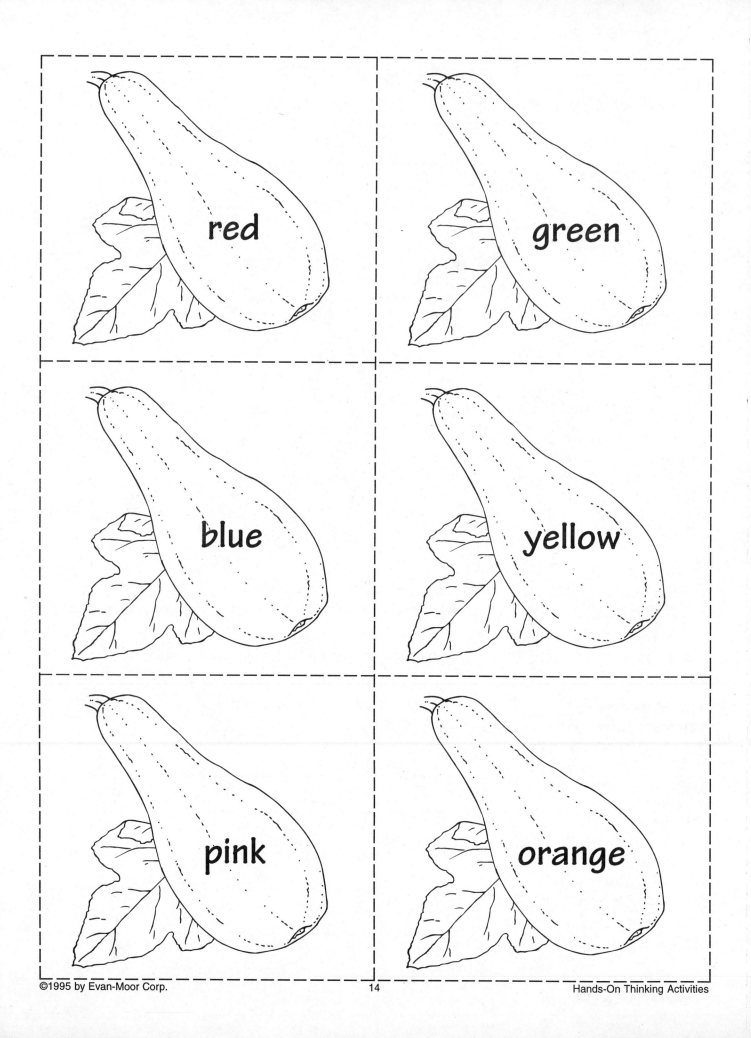

red

green

blue

yellow

pink

orange

Note: Reproduce this sign to place on the table to identify each center.

fold

Sensible
Squash

Hands-On Thinking Activities

Thinking Skills- predicting, estimating
Number of students at this center - up to 4
Time required at center - 25 minutes

Student Task

Students make predictions about certain attributes of their pumpkins.

Materials

- a collection of small pumpkins of various sizes
- a balance and gram masses (or a scale)
- string, scissors, metric rulers
- a bucket of water, paper towels
- a calculator (optional)
- center sign on page 18
- copies of the student record sheet on page 17

Teacher Notes

1. Students will select one pumpkin each. They will make predictions about their pumpkin in these areas: weight, circumference, number of lines, cost per gram, and ability to float. Students will do research to determine how close they came.

2. Students will use the string to measure the circumference of their pumpkin. They need to wrap the string around the widest part, cut it to fit, then measure the length of string using the ruler.

3. The materials at this center are shared by all the students.

For the Whiz Kid

He/She picks another gourd, and using the knowledge of their first choice, makes CLOSER predictions and record results on the back of their student record sheet.

Petite Pumpkins

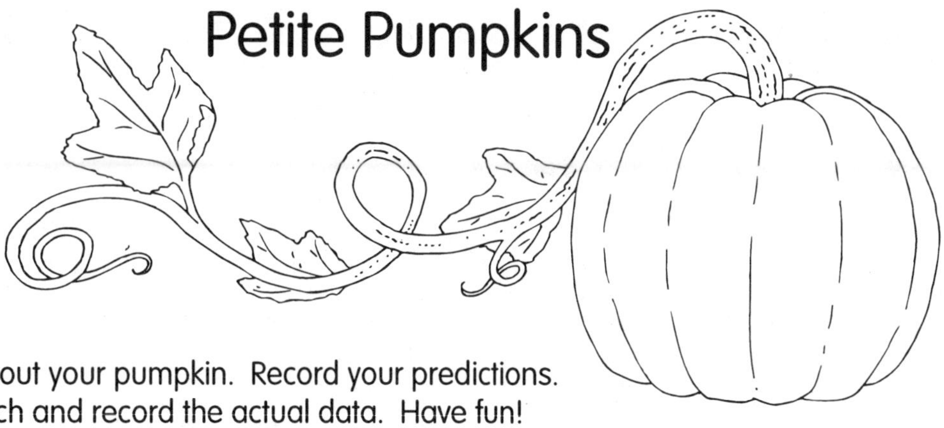

Make predictions about your pumpkin. Record your predictions.
Then do your research and record the actual data. Have fun!

	Prediction	Actual
1. How much does your pumpkin weigh?	_____	_____
2. What is the circumference of your pumpkin?	_____	_____
3. How many lines does your pumpkin have around it?	_____	_____
4. If your pumpkin cost $.02 per gram, how much would it cost?	_____	_____
5. Will your pumpkin float?	_____	_____
6. What is the total weight of all the pumpkins at your center?	_____	_____

7. List four attributes that make these pumpkins different from each other.

_____

_____

_____

_____

Note: Reproduce this sign to place on the table to identify each center.

fold

Petite
Pumpkins

18   Hands-On Thinking Activities

Thinking Skill - designing, following directions
Number of students at this center - up to 4
Time required at center - 25 minutes

Student Task

How many different patterns can students create on a 16-block grid using one each of four different kinds of nuts?

Materials

- four nuts per student
- container for storing nuts
- copies of the student record sheet on page 20
- center sign on page 21

Teacher Notes

1. Students can work independently at this center or can be encouraged to work cooperatively. They are to find at least six patterns using the grid on their record sheet.

2. There are many solutions to this puzzle. Students can work on finding them as long as time permits. Have students put these solutions on the back of their student record sheet.

The Nut Cache

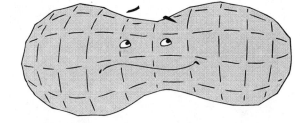

1. Take four nuts from the container.
   You need one of each kind.
2. Place each nut in a square.
   Make sure there is only one nut in each
   column down and each row across.
3. Record your pattern below. Then try again.
   See how many ways you can solve this puzzle.

1	2	3	4
5	6	7	8
9	10	11	12
13	14	15	16

The nuts are in boxes:

First try: _____ _____ _____ _____

Second try: _____ _____ _____ _____

Third try: _____ _____ _____ _____

Fourth try: _____ _____ _____ _____

Fifth try: _____ _____ _____ _____

Sixth try: _____ _____ _____ _____

Note: Reproduce this sign to place on the table to identify each center.

fold

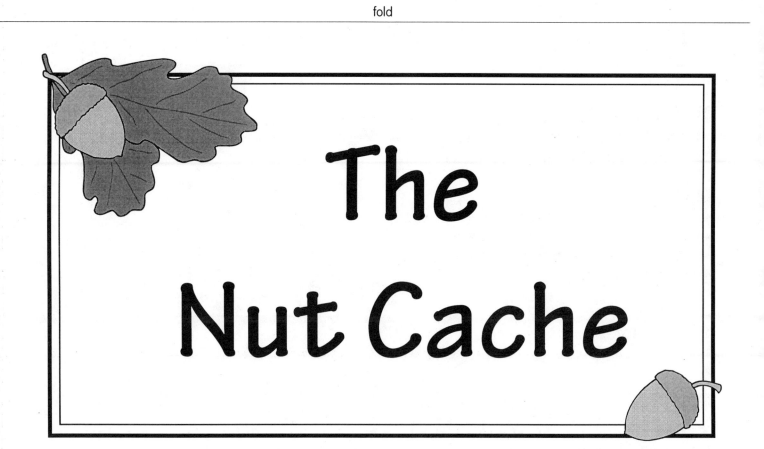

The Nut Cache

Hands-On Thinking Activities

Thinking Skills - sorting, organizing
Number of students at this center - up to 4
Time required at center - 25 minutes

The Candy Counter

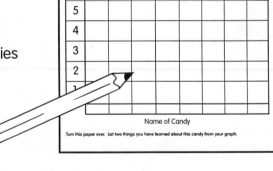

Student Task

Students will sort a variety of candies into like kinds and record the data on a graph.

Materials

- plastic bags with assorted individually-wrapped candies
- plastic bags of crayons: up to 10 colors
- copies of the student record sheet on page 23
- center sign on page 24

Teacher Notes

1. You should have up to ten varieties of candy with differing numbers of each kind in each baggie.

2. Decide in advance if your students will be able to keep their bags of candy when the activity is over.

3. Extend this activity by having students record on the back of the record sheet information that can be learned from their graph.

The Candy Counter

Dump the bag of candy on the table.
Sort it into piles of like kinds of candy.
Make a graph below that shows what is in this bag.

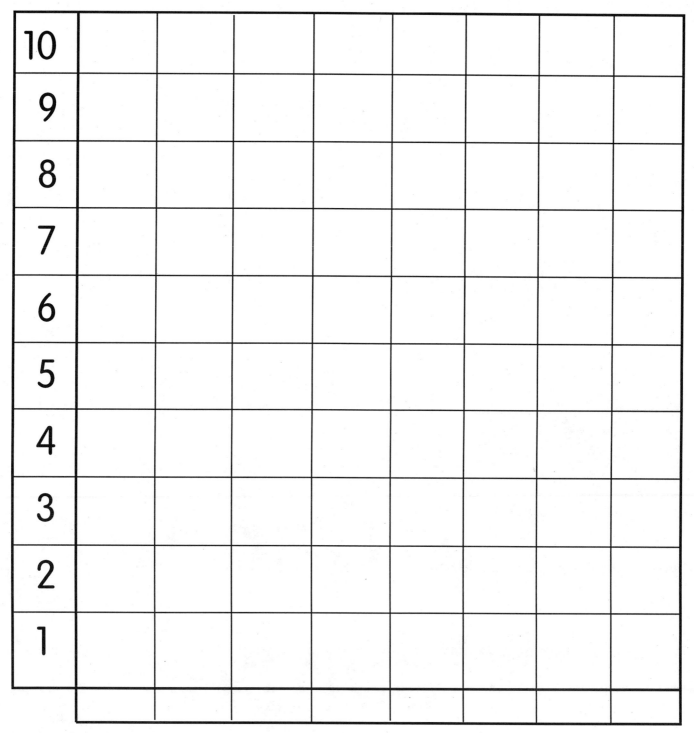

10							
9							
8							
7							
6							
5							
4							
3							
2							
1							

Name of Candy

Turn this paper over. List two things you have learned about this candy from your graph.

Hands-On Thinking Activities

Note: Reproduce this sign to place on the table to identify each center.

fold

The Candy Counter

Thinking Skills - *designing, following directions*
Number of students at this center - *up to 4*
Time required at center - *25 minutes*

Student Task

Students use their imaginations to create a variety of interesting
jack-o'-lantern faces. They will then write about the characters they have created.

Materials

If you are using the center for
drawing pumpkin faces:
• crayons, felt markers, colored pencils
• glitter
• student record sheet on page 26
• center sign on page 28

If you are using real pumpkins at the center:
• miniature pumpkins - 1 per child
• felt tip markers
• small beads, colored paper,
  curly ribbon, various seeds, buttons, etc.
• white glue
• student record sheet on page 27
• center sign on page 28

Teacher Notes

1. You can usually get a good price on these miniature pumpkins if you tell the retailer you are a teacher.
The jack-o'-lanterns are NOT carved, just decorated with a variety of materials. Turn students loose to
use their imaginations.

2. Gluing Hint: Put a small dab of glue on the pumpkin and let it sit for at least 3-4 minutes before
applying the decoration. This will give the glue time to become tacky and will hold the decoration successfully.

Jack-o'-lantern Jamboree

name _____

Design three jack-o'-lantern faces.
Make sure they all look different and interesting!
Give each one a name and write a few sentences
that tell about your new pumpkin friends!

Jack-o'-lantern Jamboree

Choose a miniature pumpkin and materials to create your own jack-o'-lantern.
Be creative! Give it a name and write about your new friend.

jack-o'-lantern's
name:

Note: Reproduce this sign to place on the table to identify each center.

fold

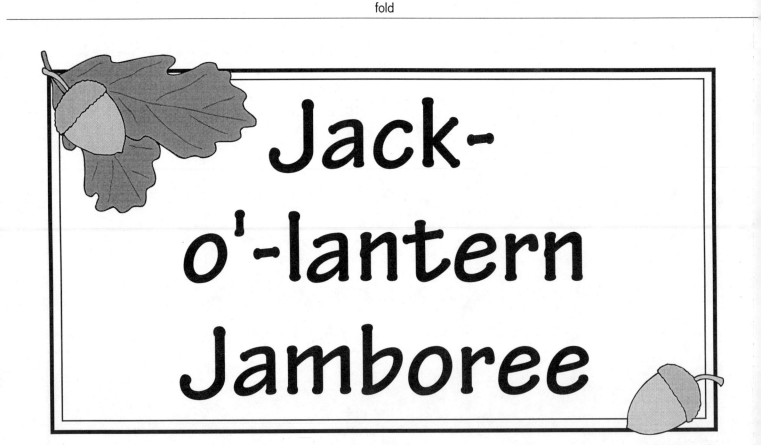

Jack-
o'-lantern
Jamboree

28

Hands-On Thinking Activities

Thinking Skills - *estimating, following directions*
Number of students at this center - *1*
Time required at center - *25 minutes*

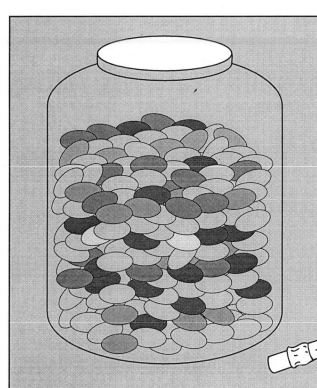

The Sweet Tooth Jar

Take a CAREFUL look at this jar filled with candy. Spend at least 6 minutes studying it from every angle. You can pick it up and look underneath too! Try to **estimate** the number of candies in this jar. Don't just guess, use logic to figure out how many pieces there are. Write your estimate below.

My **Best** estimate is: _____ candies

Tell me HOW you arrived at your number!! Explain it completely.

Explanation of estimate:

Student Task

Part One

Students estimate the number of candies in the jar. Then they are to write a complete explanation on how they arrived at their estimation. The teacher chooses the three closest estimations and reads them to the class. The class votes on the clearest explanation.

Part Two

Students experience further practice in estimation.

Materials

• center sign on page 32

Part One

• a jar of small candies
• record sheet on page 30

Part Two

• 2 empty jars, different sizes
• marbles - enough to fill the largest jar (not more than 100)
• a copy of the student record sheet on page 31

Teacher Notes

1. Be sure students understand that a "complete" explanation must be logical, thorough and sequential.

2. The teacher needs to decide ahead of time if the jar of candy will be given as a prize to the person who writes the best explanation.

Take a CAREFUL look at this jar filled with candy. Spend at least 6 minutes studying it from every angle. You can pick it up and look underneath too! Try to **estimate** the number of candies in this jar. Don't just guess, use logic to figure out how many pieces there are. Write your estimate below.

My **best** estimate is: _____ candies

NOW! Tell me HOW you arrived at your number! Explain it completely.

Explanation of estimate:

_____

_____

_____

_____

_____

_____

The Sweet Tooth Jar

Part Two

Now, take a close look at empty jar Number 1 and the bag of objects next to it. Make an estimate — how many of these objects do you think will fit into the jar? Record your estimate below and then fill up the jar, counting the number of objects it takes.

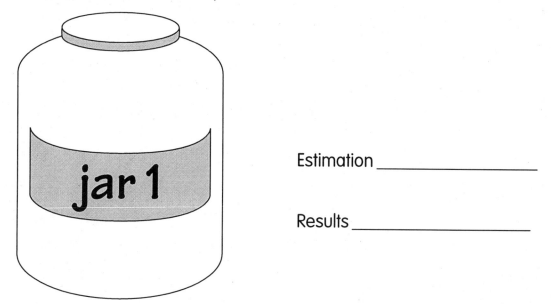

Estimation _____

Results _____

Empty the jar, and take a look at jar Number 2. Knowing what you now know, how many of these objects will it take to fill jar Number 2? Remember your results from the first jar. Record your prediction and then fill up jar Number 2. How did you do?

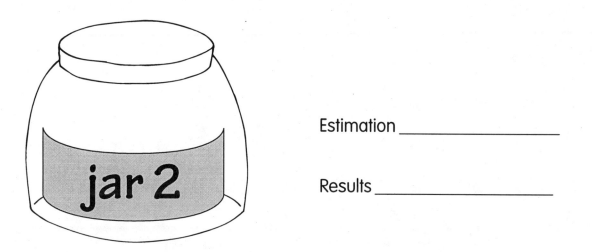

Estimation _____

Results _____

Do you want to go back now to your estimation of THE SWEET TOOTH JAR and change anything you wrote? Good luck!

 Hands-On Thinking Activities

Note: Reproduce this sign to place on the table to identify each center.

fold

The
Sweet
Tooth Jar

Hands-On Thinking Activities

Thinking Skills- predicting, interpreting
Number of students at this center - up to 4
Time required at center - 25 minutes

Drop by Drop

Drop by Drop

I hope you have a steady hand for this one. You'll need it!

Just how many drops of water do you think you can put on top of the small coin? First, make a prediction and then go to it with your eyedropper. Do it slowly so you can keep track of the number of drops! Try the experiment twice to check your results! If you try the bigger coin will your results change?

My prediction   the Actual

Small Coin

Trial Number One _____
Trial Number Two

Large Coin

Trial Number One
Trial Number Two

What surprised you about this experiment?

Why do you think you can get so much water on a small coin?

25   10

Student Task
Children predict how many drops of water will remain on a coin.
They experiment to find out how close they came.

Materials
- two sizes of foil-covered chocolate coins
  (or use real coins)
- containers of water
- eyedroppers
- paper towels under each student work area
- a trash can (for wet towels at clean-up time)
- copies of the student record sheet on page 34
- center sign on page 35

Teacher Notes
1. Things will get wet in this center, so provide plenty of paper towels.

2. Extend this activity by having children repeat this experiment to see if the same results occur. If not, ask them to explain why.

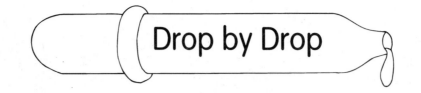

Drop by Drop

I hope you have a steady hand for this one. You'll need it!

Just how many drops of water do you think you can put on top of the small coin? First, make a prediction and then go to it with your eyedropper. Do it slowly so you can keep track of the number of drops! Try the experiment twice to check your results! If you try the bigger coin will your results change? Try it and see.

	My prediction	The Actual Number
Small Coin		
Trial Number One	_____	_____
Trial Number Two	_____	_____
Large Coin		
Trial Number One	_____	_____
Trial Number Two	_____	_____

What surprised you about this experiment?

_____

_____

Why do you think you can get so much water on a small coin?

_____

_____

Note: Reproduce this sign to place on the table to identify each center.

fold

35

Thinking Skill - *sorting, following directions*
Number of students at this center - *2*
Time required at center - *25 minutes*

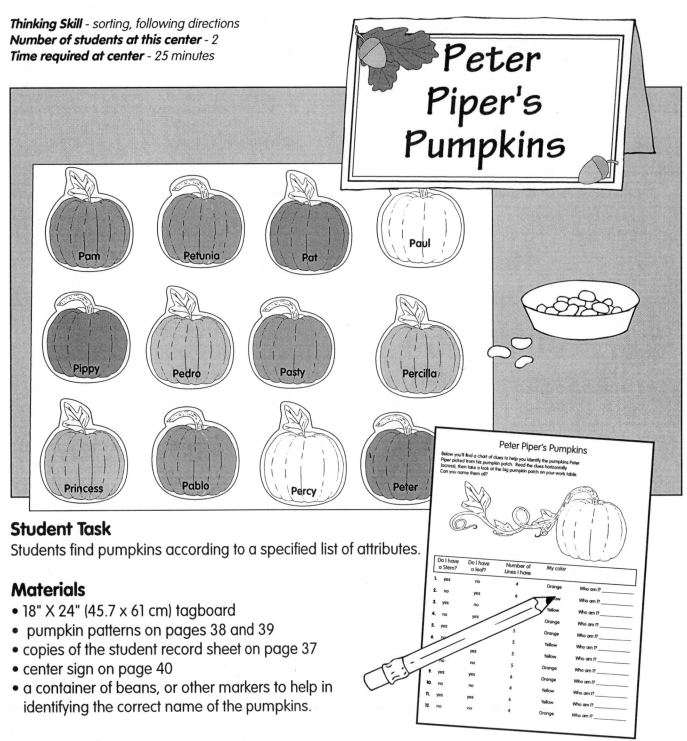

Student Task
Students find pumpkins according to a specified list of attributes.

Materials
- 18" X 24" (45.7 x 61 cm) tagboard
- pumpkin patterns on pages 38 and 39
- copies of the student record sheet on page 37
- center sign on page 40
- a container of beans, or other markers to help in identifying the correct name of the pumpkins.

Teacher Notes
1. Prepare the pumpkin display by coloring and cutting out the 12 pumpkins on pages 38 and 39. Arrange them randomly on a piece of colorful tagboard, and laminate. Place the display on the table where the students will be working.

2. Some students will need to put "counters" or beans on the pumpkins fitting the attribute being described. This helps them to identify only those pumpkins that should continue to be judged. As they come across an attribute that does not fit that particular pumpkin, all beans are removed from it. By systematically going through each attribute, they should be able to locate the correct pumpkin and write its name on their record sheets.

Peter Piper's Pumpkins

Below you'll find a chart of clues to help you identify the pumpkins Peter Piper picked from his pumpkin patch. Read the clues horizontally (across), then take a look at the big pumpkin patch on your work table. Can you name them all?

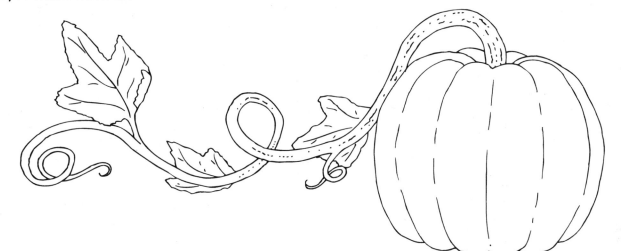

	Do I have a stem?	Do I have a leaf?	Number of lines I have	My color	
1.	yes	no	4	Orange	Who am I? _____
2.	no	yes	6	Yellow	Who am I? _____
3.	yes	no	4	Yellow	Who am I? _____
4.	no	yes	6	Orange	Who am I? _____
5.	yes	no	5	Orange	Who am I? _____
6.	no	yes	5	Yellow	Who am I? _____
7.	yes	yes	5	Yellow	Who am I? _____
8.	no	no	5	Orange	Who am I? _____
9.	yes	yes	6	Orange	Who am I? _____
10.	no	no	4	Yellow	Who am I? _____
11.	yes	yes	6	Yellow	Who am I? _____
12.	no	no	4	Orange	Who am I? _____

Hands-On Thinking Activities

Teacher: Color the pumpkins before placing them in the center.

Color this orange.

Color this yellow.

Color this yellow.

Color this orange.

Color this orange.

Color this yellow.

Peter

Percilla

Paul

Pam

Petunia

Pat

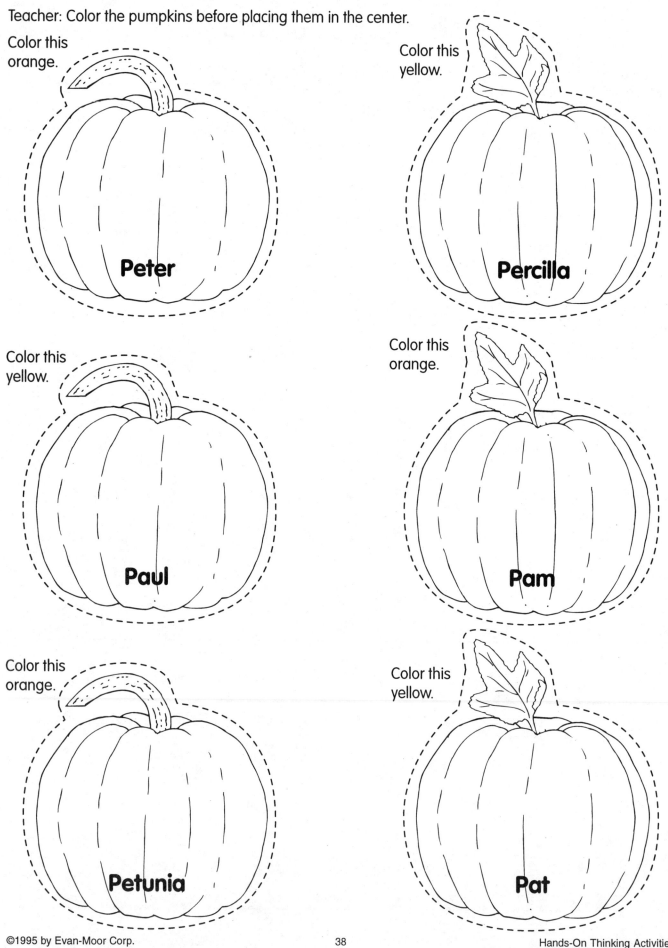

Hands-On Thinking Activities

Color this
yellow.

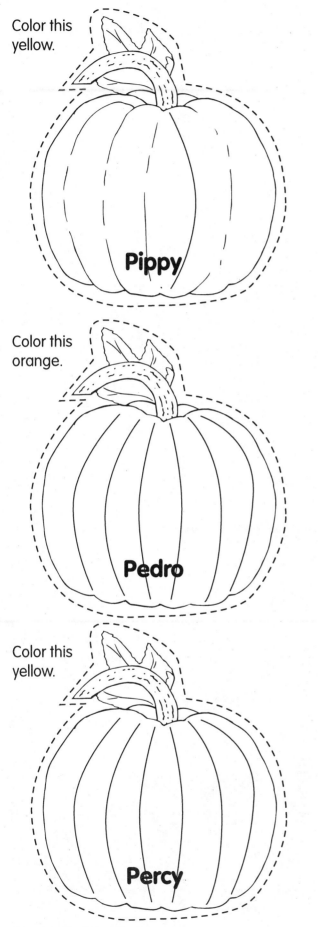

Pippy

Color this
orange.

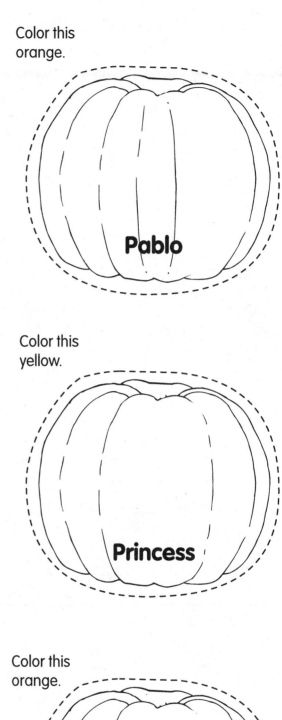

Pablo

Color this
orange.

Pedro

Color this
yellow.

Princess

Color this
yellow.

Percy

Color this
orange.

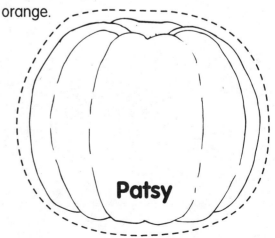

Patsy

Hands-On Thinking Activities

Note: Reproduce this sign to place on the table to identify each center.

fold

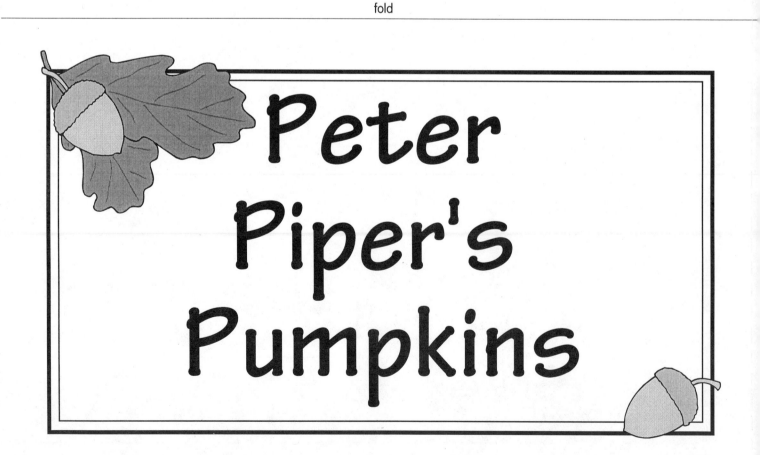

Peter Piper's Pumpkins

40

Thinking Skills - *predicting, following directions*
Number of students at this center - *up to 4*
Time required at center - *25 minutes*

Student Task

Students will build two-and-three-dimensional shapes out of gumdrops and toothpicks to use as bubble-blowing devices. They dip the device in the soap mixture, and predict what shape of bubble will be made when they blow through the form.

Materials

- a gallon (3.8 liters) of bubble solution
- eight small gum drops per student
- twelve toothpicks per student
- a spool of thread, scissors
- copies of the student record sheet on page 42
- center sign on page 43
- a large roll of paper towels, sponges
- newspapers
- large containers {at least 5" (13 cm) in diameter}
- garbage can (for wet newspapers and paper towels)

Soap Mixture: *1 gallon (3.8 liters) of water and 1 cup (250 ml) of soap and 1/8 cup (30 ml) glycerin. Try making a bubble. If it breaks too fast, add a bit more liquid dish soap.* **Ivory** *makes a stronger bubble than other brands.*

Teacher Notes

1. A volunteer would be helpful in this center. A parent can help keep the students on task and rotating through in a timely manner. Once students get to this center, they tend to stay forever.

2. Plan on this being a very popular and WET center. Cover the table with newspapers. You will want to replace them frequently to keep the mess under control! Place a garbage can by each student test area. Have students keep their work folders someplace where they won't get wet.

3. Have students begin with two-dimensional shapes, as this works best. Then try making three-dimensional shapes. As students try new shapes, have them use the same gum drops.

4. You can buy glycerin at most drugstores.

Bubble Magic

Can you predict where you'll find a bubble and what shape it will be? Follow the diagrams below and build a shape that interests you. Use toothpicks and gum drops.

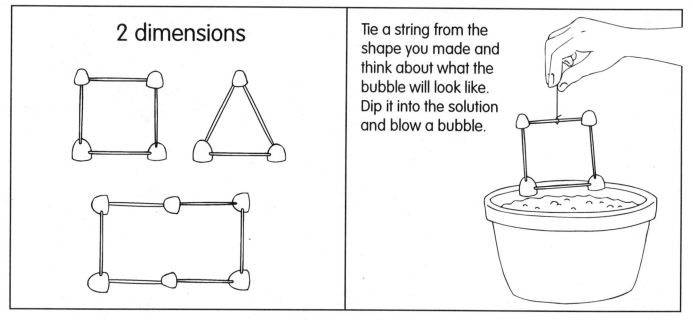

2 dimensions

Tie a string from the shape you made and think about what the bubble will look like. Dip it into the solution and blow a bubble.

- What bubble shapes could be made out of a square?
- What can you make from a rectangle?

_____

_____

_____

Add to your form to make it three-dimensional. Dip it and blow.

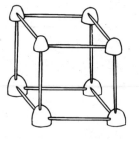

What bubble shapes can be made out of a cube?

_____

_____

_____

_____

List three things you learned from the bubbles you created.

1. _____

2. _____

3. _____

Note: Reproduce this sign to place on the table to identify each center.

fold

Bubble Magic

43

Hands-On Thinking Activities

Winter Activities

	Following Directions	Predicting	Estimating	Interpreting	Sorting	Classifying	Organizing	Designing
Marshmallow Madness			❄	❄				
Doling Out the Dough	❄							
Creative Creations	❄							❄
Glorious Gifts		❄	❄				❄	
Cool Climates				❄				
Winter Line-Up				❄			❄	
Squishy Squares!							❄	❄
Puzzling Presents				❄			❄	❄
The Great Glove Game				❄				
Winter Wonderland	❄							❄

Note: Provide this reproducible for any students who finish a center early.

Name It	an animal	something to eat	a country	something to wear	a girl's name
EXAMPLE: **A**	anteater	artichoke	Australia	anklets	Anna
W					
I					
N					
T					
E					
R					

Hands-On Thinking Activities

Thinking Skills - *estimating, interpreting*
Number of students at this center - *1*
Time required at center - *25 minutes*

Marshmallow Madness

Marshmallow Madness

Take a CAREFUL look at this jar filled with marshmallows. Spend at least 5 minutes studying it from every angle. You can pick it up and look underneath too! Try to **estimate** the number of marshmallows in this jar. Don't just guess. Use some logic to figure out how many pieces there are. Write your estimate below.

My **Best** estimate is: _____ marshmallows

NOW! Tell me HOW you arrived at your number!! Ex[plain] [com]pletely.

Explanation of estimate: _____

_____

_____

_____

_____

_____

Estimate how many words can you make using letters from the word MARSHMALLOW? Write them on the back!

| my estimate | result |

Student Task

Students estimate the number of marshmallows in the jar. Then they are to write a complete explanation on how they arrived at their estimation. The teacher chooses the three closest estimations and reads them to the class. The class votes on the clearest explanation.

Materials

- a jar of small marshmallows
- student record sheet on page 47
- center sign on page 48

Teacher Notes

1. Be sure students understand that a "complete" explanation must be logical, thorough, and sequential.

2. The teacher needs to decide ahead of time if the jar of marshmallows will be given as a prize to the person who writes the best explanation.

Marshmallow Madness

Take a CAREFUL look at this jar filled with marshmallows. Spend at least five minutes studying it from every angle. You can pick it up and look underneath, too! Try to **estimate** the number of marshmallows in this jar. Don't just guess. Use some logic to figure out how many pieces there are. Write your estimate below.

My **best** estimate is: _____ marshmallows

NOW! Tell me HOW you arrived at your number! Explain it completely.

Explanation of estimate: _____

_____

_____

_____

_____

Estimate how many words you can make using letters from the word MARSHMALLOW. Write them on the back!

my estimate	result

Note: Reproduce this sign to place on the table to identify each center.

fold

Marshmallow Madness

Hands-On Thinking Activities

Thinking Skill - following directions
Number of students at this center - up to 4
Time required at center - 25 minutes

Student Task

Students follow a recipe to mix a dough to be used in other activities.

Materials

- for each student:
  - 1 cup (250 ml) flour
  - 1/4 cup (60 ml) salt
  - 6 tablespoons (90 ml) water
  - a mixing bowl
  - wooden spoon
  - measuring cups
  - extra flour for kneading
- copies of the student record sheet on page 50
- center sign on page 51

Doling Out the Dough

Winter is a time for cooking! Here's a chance to cook — but **not** to eat! This dough will make several works of art that you can hang on a tree or in your room at home.

Art Dough

In your mixing bowl, combine:
- 1 cup (250 ml) flour
- 1/4 cup (60 ml) salt
- 6 Tablespoons (90 ml) water

Steps to follow:
1. Mix well with the spoon.

2. When the dough begins to come away from the sides of the bowl, form it into a ball. Spread a little flour on the table top. Place the ball of dough on the floured surface.

3. Knead the dough for 5 minutes. If the dough is too dry, add a few drops of water. When the dough is smooth to the touch it will be ready.

When you are finished, take your dough over to the "Creative Creations" center to make your work of art!

Draw a picture of what you made with the Art Dough.

Teacher Notes

1. Have the flour, salt, and water in open containers on the table. Leave the table uncovered, as it makes a good surface for kneading the dough. Have children add a bit of water or flour to the dough as needed when they are kneading the dough.

2. Knead the dough for at least five minutes until it has a smooth, silky surface. Demonstrate to the class how to knead dough.

3. When the dough is completed, students are to take it to the "Creative Creations" center for the next step.

Doling Out the Dough

Winter is a time for cooking! Here's a chance to cook — but **not** to eat! This dough will make several works of art that you can hang on a tree or in your room at home.

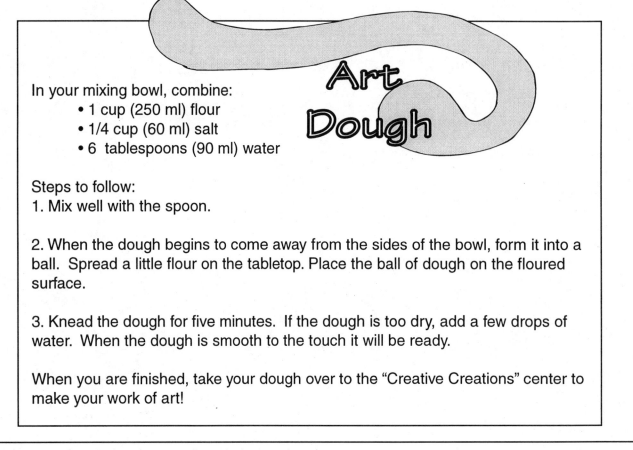

In your mixing bowl, combine:
- 1 cup (250 ml) flour
- 1/4 cup (60 ml) salt
- 6 tablespoons (90 ml) water

Steps to follow:

1. Mix well with the spoon.

2. When the dough begins to come away from the sides of the bowl, form it into a ball. Spread a little flour on the tabletop. Place the ball of dough on the floured surface.

3. Knead the dough for five minutes. If the dough is too dry, add a few drops of water. When the dough is smooth to the touch it will be ready.

When you are finished, take your dough over to the "Creative Creations" center to make your work of art!

Draw a picture of what you made with the art dough.

Note: Reproduce this sign to place on the table to identify each center.

fold

Doling Out the Dough

Thinking Skill - designing, following directions
Number of students at this center - up to 4
Time required at center - 25 minutes

Creative
Creations

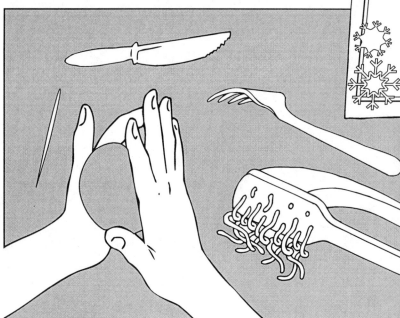

Creative Creations

• Make sure your dough is smooth and not sticky. Knead it a few more minutes if necessary.

• Store your ball of dough on one of your pieces of foil at the table. When you start creating your work of art, do it on your other piece of foil. If you don't work on the foil, the dough will stick and ruin your object when you try to lift it off the table.

• Use the tools at the table to decorate one or more objects.

• When you have finished, write your name on the foil with a black marker.

• Put your creation in the container your teacher has provided.

Helpful hints:

1. When attaching one piece of dough to another piece, scratch the surfaces with a tooth pick and place a tiny bit of water there to help the two pieces "stick" together.

2. If your object is too thin, it will tend to burn while being cooked in the oven.

3. Try to keep your object the same thickness all over.

4. Use the garlic press to make beards and curly hair.

Student Task

Students use the dough made in the **Doling Out the Dough** center to create small decorative objects.

Materials

• clay dough
• a selection of tools such as:

toothpicks	plastic knives
garlic press	sharp pencils
plastic forks	straws, etc.

• aluminum foil
• small cup of water
• permanent black marker
• a paper clip for each student
• plastic bags for students who want to take their extra dough home
• copies of the student record sheet on page 53
• center sign on page 54
• shallow boxes (so you can take creations home to bake)

Dough Art Cooking Instructions:
The trick here is to cook the dough art as slowly as possible, so the pieces stay pale in color. Place them on the foil squares right on the oven rack. It works best to cook the dough art in a gas oven, at the lowest temperature, from 2 to 8 hours, depending on the thickness of the pieces. Check often for doneness (pieces will be hard to the touch). If you have a strong pilot light, you can just put them in an oven overnight without even turning it on!

Teacher Notes

1. Cut the foil into about 4" (10 cm) squares. Make enough for two pieces per student. Students work directly on the foil so the dough will be ready to cook in the oven.

2. Students use the tools to add details and decorations to the dough ornaments. If the pieces are to be hung, stick a paper clip in the dough to create a loop for a hook or ribbon.

3. The finished pieces can be hung on a tree or used as gifts.

Creative Creations

• Make sure your dough is smooth and not sticky. Knead it a few more minutes if necessary.

• Store your ball of dough on one of your pieces of foil at the table. When you start creating your work of art, do it on your other piece of foil. If you don't work on the foil, the dough will stick and ruin your object when you try to lift it off the table.

• Use the tools at the table to decorate one or more objects.

• When you have finished, write your name on the foil with a black marker.

• Put your creation in the container your teacher has provided.

Helpful hints:

1. When attaching one piece of dough to another piece, scratch the surfaces with a toothpick and place a tiny bit of water there to help the two pieces "stick" together.

2. If your object is too thin, it will tend to burn while being cooked in the oven.

3. Try to keep your object the same thickness all over.

4. Use the garlic press to make beards and curly hair.

5. Press a paper clip into the top of the finished work of art if you want to hang it up later.

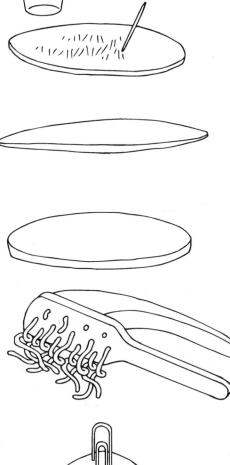

Note: Reproduce this sign to place on the table to identify each center.

fold

Creative
Creations

Thinking Skills - *predicting, estimating, organizing*
Number of students at this center - *up to 4*
Time required at center - *25 minutes*

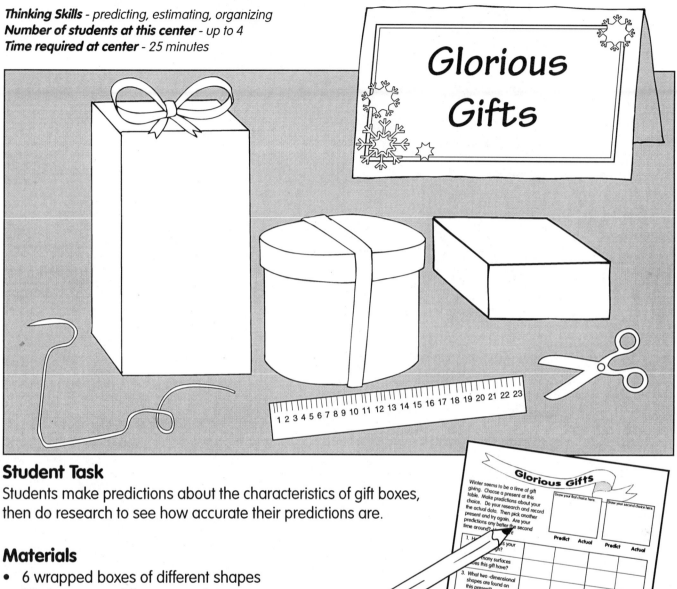

Student Task

Students make predictions about the characteristics of gift boxes, then do research to see how accurate their predictions are.

Materials

- 6 wrapped boxes of different shapes filled to create different weights
- string
- scissors
- metric rulers
- balance scale and mass weights
- copies of the student record sheet on page 56
- center sign on page 57

Teacher Notes

1. Identify each present with a name or number. Try to include boxes of various three-dimensional geometric shapes.

2. Each student will be making predictions and verifying information about the boxes on the table.

3. Extend the activity by challenging the students to take one of the gifts and draw a pattern on the back of the student record sheet to show the shape of the box if it was cut along its edges and laid flat.

Glorious Gifts

Winter seems to be a time of gift giving. Choose a present at this table. Make predictions about your choice.   Do your research and record the actual data. Then pick another present and try again. Are your predictions any better the second time around? Have fun!

Draw your first choice here.

Draw your second choice here.

	Predict	Actual	Predict	Actual
1. How much does your present weigh?				
2. How many surfaces does this gift have?				
3. What two -dimensional shapes are found on this present?				
4. What is the distance around the widest part?				
5. Estimate how much they would weigh if you had ten the same size.				

6. Consider the weight and shape of each present. What could be inside?

   first present _____   second present _____

7. List three attributes that describe how the presents at this table are different.

   1. _____

   2. _____

   3. _____

Note: Reproduce this sign to place on the table to identify each center.

fold

Glorious
Gifts

Thinking Skill - *interpreting*
Number of students at this center - *up to 4*
Time required at center - *25 minutes*

Cool Climates

World Atlas

Student Task
Students will compare the lowest temperatures in eight cities around the world with the local temperature and calculate an average.

Materials
- copies of the current newspaper clipping for national and international weather
- clear plastic pocket sheets to protect newspaper clippings
- copies of the student record sheet on page 59
- copies of the graph form on page 60
- center sign on page 61
- atlas

Teacher Notes

1. Place the weather reports in the plastic pocket sheets. Find out the lowest temperature for your city on this day.

2. Students record the data from the weather reports on their record sheets (page 59), then graph the data (page 60).

3. Students will need to know how to find an average temperature.

4. Extend this activity by having students record data for the hottest temperatures found on this day.

> ***Averaging***: *Add all the data and then divide that answer by how many numbers were used.*

Cool Climates

How does your weather compare to other places in the world? Do some research and record the data for the following questions. Then graph your data.

Record the eight cities with the lowest temperatures listed for

_____
Month, Day, Year

city	state/province/country	temperature

1. What is the average low temperature of these eight cities?

2. What was today's low temperature in your city?

3. How many degrees different is this average from your town's low for this day?

How to figure an average:
Add all the data and then divide that answer by how many numbers were used.

44 + 32 + 12 + 7 + 25 = 120

120 divided by 5 = 24

Cool Climates Weather Graph

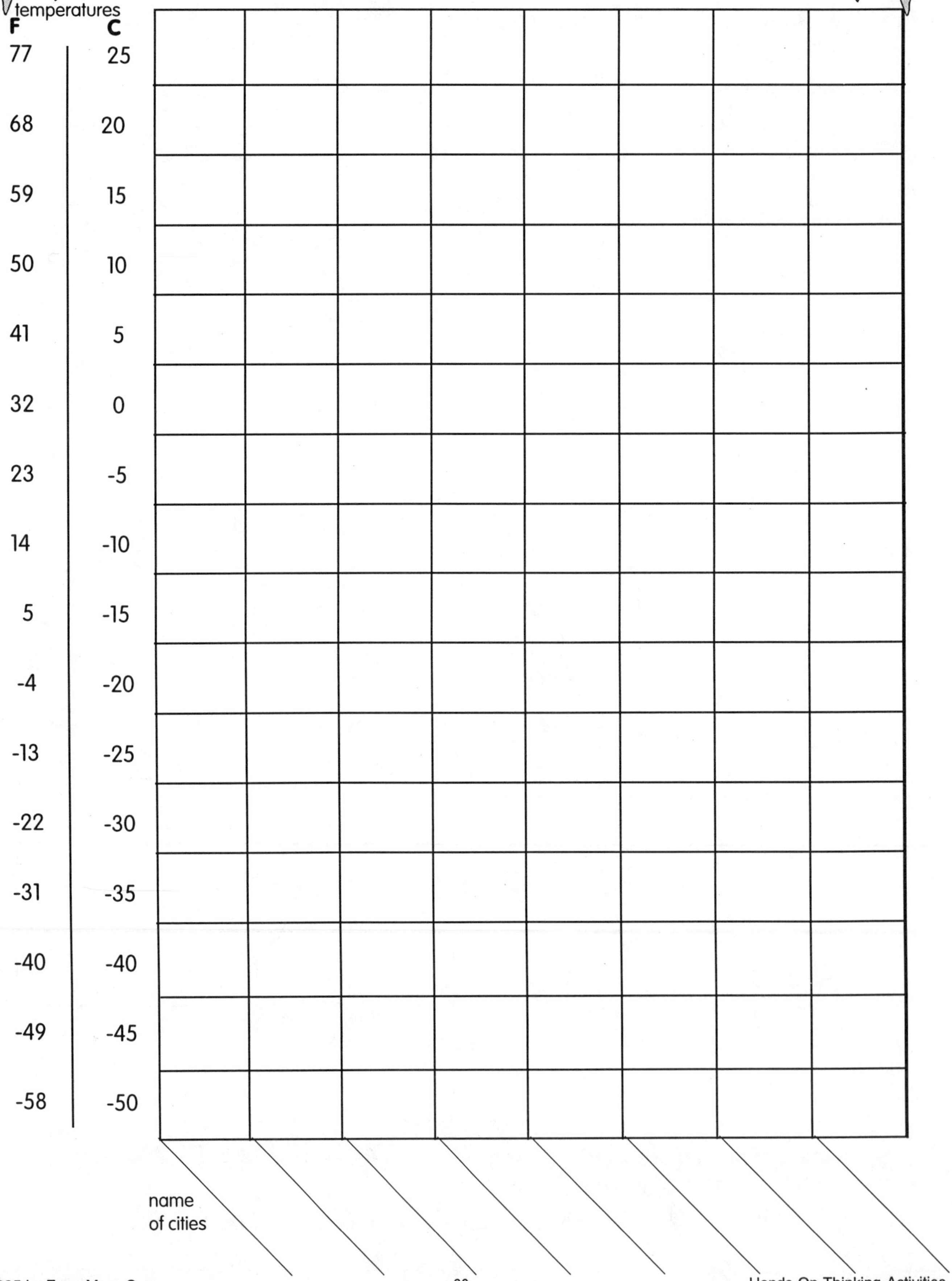

temperatures	
F	**C**
77	25
68	20
59	15
50	10
41	5
32	0
23	-5
14	-10
5	-15
-4	-20
-13	-25
-22	-30
-31	-35
-40	-40
-49	-45
-58	-50

name
of cities

Hands-On Thinking Activities

Note: Reproduce this sign to place on the table to identify each center.

fold

Cool Climates

Thinking Skills - interpreting, organizing
Number of students at this center - up to 4
Time required at center - 25 minutes

Winter Line-up

Student Task
Students follow a series of clues to find the position in line of the different ice skaters.

Materials
- sets of cards (See pages 64 and 65.)
- tagboard
- envelopes for storing cards
- copies of the student record sheet on page 63
- center sign on page 66

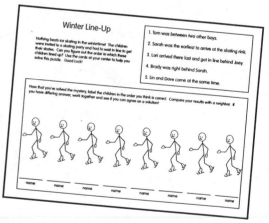

Teacher Notes
1. Cut out the cards on pages 64 and 65. Include some blank cards to use as place holders. Color the cards and glue them to tagboard. Laminate them. Place each set in an envelope.

2. Be sure students understand the process to follow in solving this type of puzzle before they begin. Help students understand that, as they read the clues, they will need to place some kind of marker to hold places for names they don't know yet. Not until the last clue will all names become evident.

For the Whiz Kid:
These students can create their own puzzle using the same cards put into a different order. Have them write their clues to this order on the back of the student record sheet; then find other students to try to solve their mystery order.

   Hands-On Thinking Activities

Winter Line-Up

Nothing beats ice skating in the wintertime! The children were invited to a skating party and had to wait in line to get their skates. Can you figure out the order in which these children lined up? Use the cards at your center to help you solve this puzzle. Good luck!

1. Tom was between two other boys.

2. Sarah was the earliest to arrive at the skating rink.

3. Lori arrived there last and got in line behind Joey.

4. Brady was right behind Sarah.

5. Lin and David came at the same time.

Now that you've solved the mystery, label the children in the order you think is correct. Compare your results with a neighbor. If you have differing answers, work together and see if you can agree on a solution!

name	name	name	name	name	name	name	name

Hands-On Thinking Activities

Lori

Joey

David

Brady

Hands-On Thinking Activities

Tom

Sarah

John

Lin

Note: Reproduce this sign to place on the table to identify each center.

fold

Winter Line-up

Hands-On Thinking Activities

Thinking Skills - organizing, designing
Number of students at this center - up to 4
Time required at center - 25 minutes

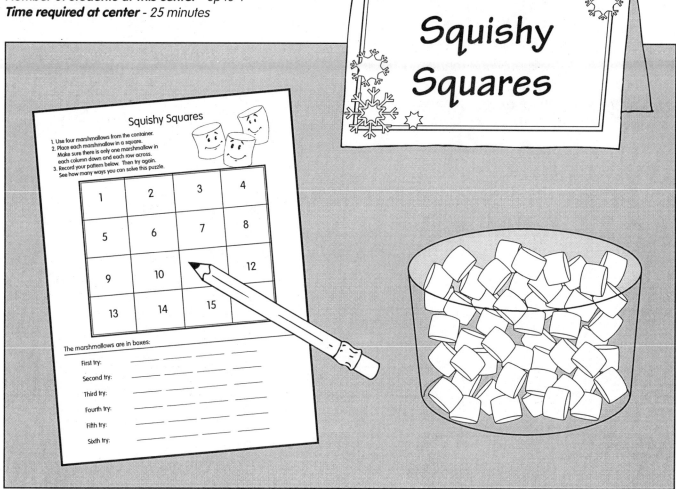

Student Task
How many different patterns can students create on a 16-block grid using four marshmallows?

Materials
• a large container of mini-marshmallows
• copies of the student record sheet on page 68
• center sign on page 69

Teacher Notes
1. Have students take four marshmallows from the container and keep them.

2. Students are to find at least six patterns using the grid on their student record sheets. There are many solutions to this puzzle. Students can work on finding them as long as time permits. Have students put these solutions on the back of their student record sheet.

For the Whiz Kid
You can make this more challenging by using colored marshmallows (or other counters) and requiring students to have different colors in each place. This extends the possible answers.

Squishy Squares

1. Use four marshmallows from the container.
2. Place each marshmallow in a square.
   Make sure there is only one marshmallow in
   each column down and each row across.
3. Record your pattern below. Then try again.
   See how many ways you can solve this puzzle.

1	2	3	4
5	6	7	8
9	10	11	12
13	14	15	16

The marshmallows are in boxes:

First try: _____ _____ _____ _____

Second try: _____ _____ _____ _____

Third try: _____ _____ _____ _____

Fourth try: _____ _____ _____ _____

Fifth try: _____ _____ _____ _____

Sixth try: _____ _____ _____ _____

Hands-On Thinking Activities

Note: Reproduce this sign to place on the table to identify each center.

fold

Squishy Squares

Thinking Skills - interpreting, organizing, designing
Number of students at this center - up to 4
Time required at center - 25 minutes

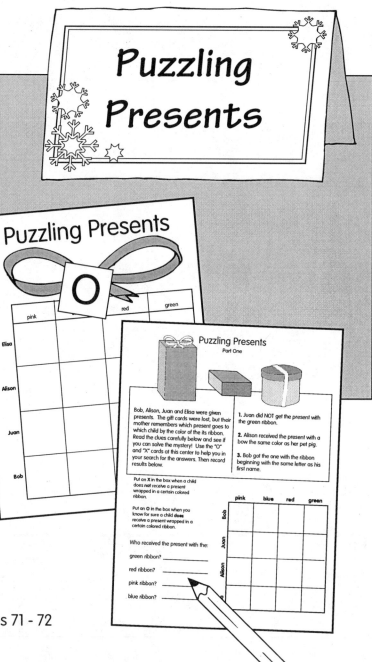

Student Task

Students use a grid to help them analyze a set of clues to determine which gift belongs to which child.

Materials

- prepared grid mats - page 73
- construction paper
- sets of X and O cards - page 74
- envelopes
- copies of the student record sheets on pages 71 - 72
- center sign on page 75

Teacher Notes

1. You will need to prepare the following materials for each student at the center:
   - grid mat - page 73
   - envelope containing **X** and **O** cards - page 74
   - copies of student record sheets - pages 71 and 72

   Adhere the grid mats to construction paper and laminate.

2. Students will use the cards to try to solve the puzzle. It is important that they follow the directions carefully. They need to place the **X** cards in squares when a child did NOT receive a present and an **O** card if the child DID receive a present. For example:

If a child received the red-ribboned gift, an **O** is placed in the box. **X** cards are placed in the other boxes after that child's name on the grid. By following this procedure, the student will end up with one **O** in each row marking the person receiving the gift.

Puzzling Presents
Part One

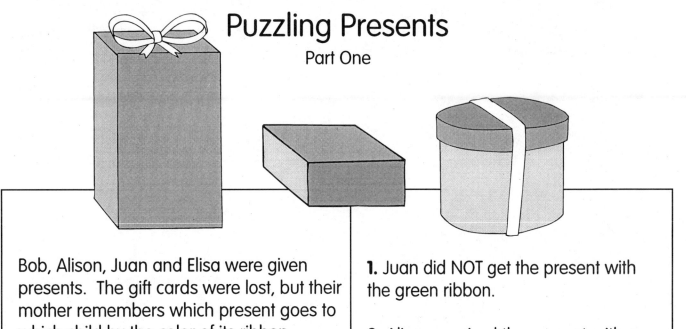

Bob, Alison, Juan and Elisa were given presents. The gift cards were lost, but their mother remembers which present goes to which child by the color of its ribbon. Read the clues carefully below and see if you can solve the mystery! Use the "O" and "X" cards at this center to help you in your search for the answers. Then record results below.

1. Juan did NOT get the present with the green ribbon.

2. Alison received the present with a bow the same color as her pet pig.

3. Bob got the one with the ribbon beginning with the same letter as his first name.

Put an **X** in the box when a child does **not** receive a present wrapped in a certain colored ribbon.

Put an **O** in the box when you know for sure a child **does** receive a present wrapped in a certain colored ribbon.

Who received the present with the:

green ribbon? _____

red ribbon? _____

pink ribbon? _____

blue ribbon? _____

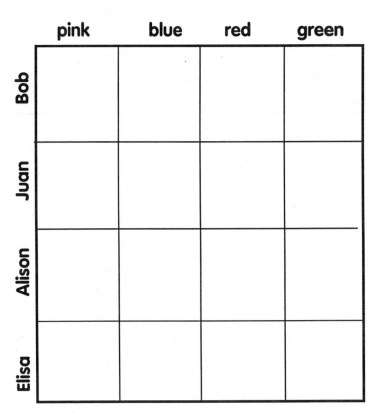

	pink	blue	red	green
Bob				
Juan				
Alison				
Elisa				

Hands-On Thinking Activities

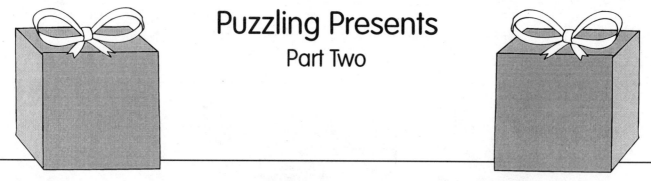

Puzzling Presents
Part Two

Now it's your turn to try and write PUZZLING PRESENT clues to try and stump your friends! Use the grid and record 4 names and 4 colors of ribbons. If you have other ideas, try them out instead!

- Put an **X** in the box when something is **not** true.

- Put an **O** in the box when something is true.

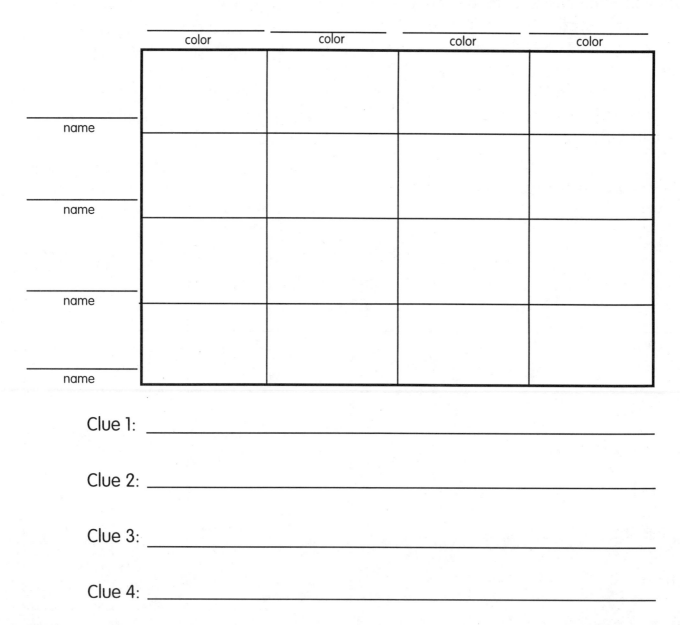

Clue 1: _____

Clue 2: _____

Clue 3: _____

Clue 4: _____

 Hands-On Thinking Activities

Puzzling Presents

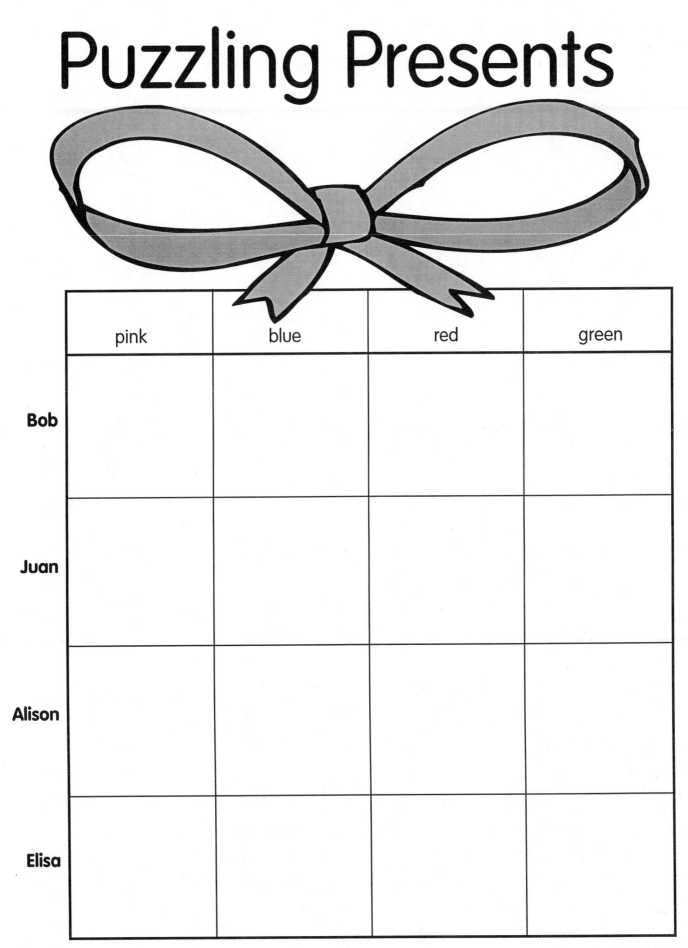

	pink	blue	red	green
Bob				
Juan				
Alison				
Elisa				

 Hands-On Thinking Activities

Puzzling Presents

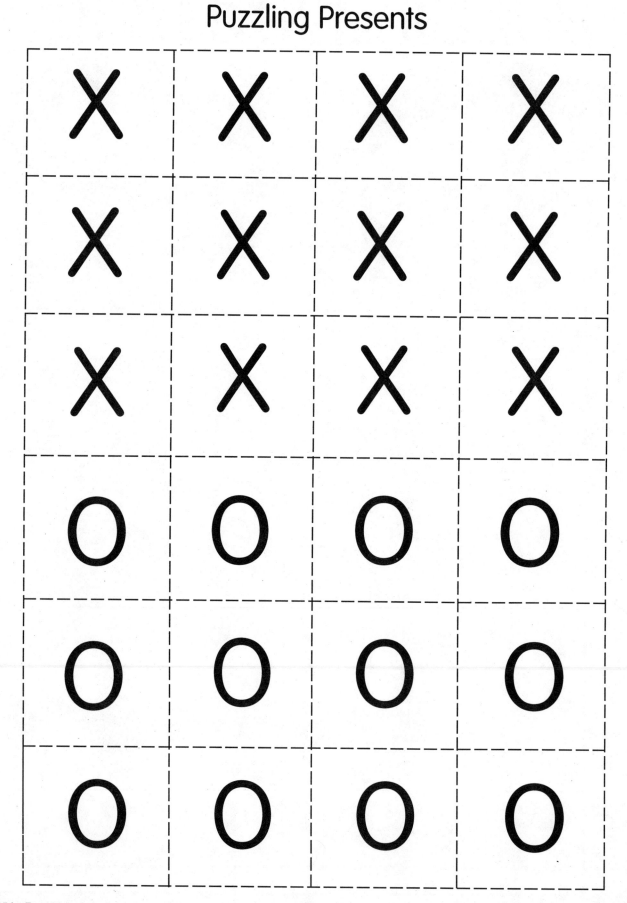

Hands-On Thinking Activities

Note: Reproduce this sign to place on the table to identify each center.

fold

Puzzling Presents

Thinking Skill - interpreting
Number of students at this center - *up to 2*
Time required at center - *25 minutes*

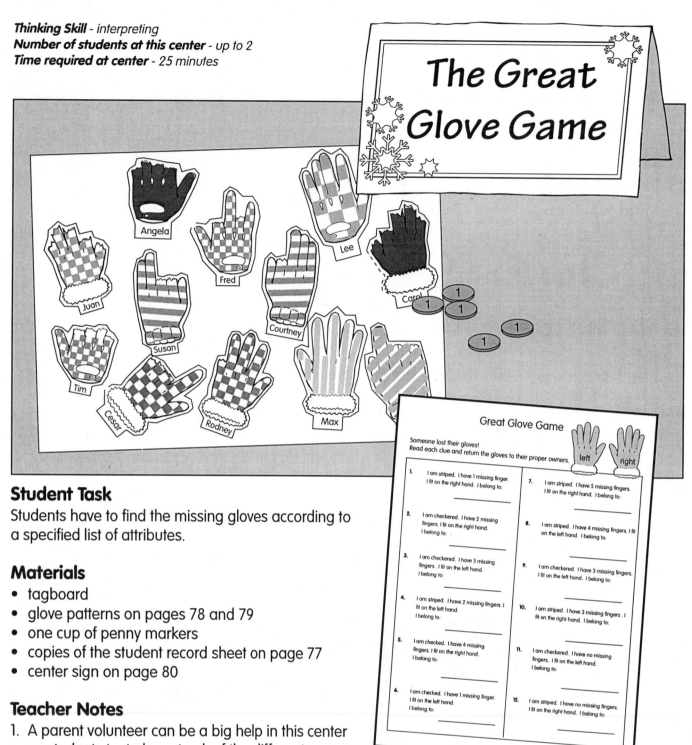

The Great Glove Game

Student Task

Students have to find the missing gloves according to a specified list of attributes.

Materials

- tagboard
- glove patterns on pages 78 and 79
- one cup of penny markers
- copies of the student record sheet on page 77
- center sign on page 80

Teacher Notes

1. A parent volunteer can be a big help in this center as students try to keep track of the different attributes of twelve gloves.

2. Prepare the Great Glove Game graphic using the patterns on pages 78 and 79. Cut out the individual gloves, glue them on a sheet of tagboard, and laminate.

3. Students can use the markers to keep track of the gloves fitting the clues. As gloves are eliminated, the markers are removed. The glove with the one remaining marker should be the correct answer. For example:

> If the first clue says "striped," a marker is put on all striped gloves. If the next clue says "one missing finger," the counters will be taken off all striped gloves that do not have one missing finger. This process continues through all of the clues.

The Great Glove Game

Someone lost their gloves!
Read each clue and return the gloves to their proper owners.

left   right

1. I am striped. I have one missing finger. I fit on the right hand. I belong to:

_____

2. I am checkered. I have two missing fingers. I fit on the right hand. I belong to:

_____

3. I am checkered. I have five missing fingers. I fit on the left hand. I belong to:

_____

4. I am striped. I have two missing fingers. I fit on the left hand. I belong to:

_____

5. I am checked. I have four missing fingers. I fit on the right hand. I belong to:

_____

6. I am checked. I have one missing finger. I fit on the left hand. I belong to:

_____

7. I am striped. I have five missing fingers. I fit on the right hand. I belong to:

_____

8. I am striped. I have four missing fingers. I fit on the left hand. I belong to:

_____

9. I am checkered. I have three missing fingers. I fit on the left hand. I belong to:

_____

10. I am striped. I have three missing fingers. I fit on the right hand. I belong to:

_____

11. I am checkered. I have no missing fingers. I fit on the left hand. I belong to:

_____

12. I am striped. I have no missing fingers. I fit on the right hand. I belong to:

_____

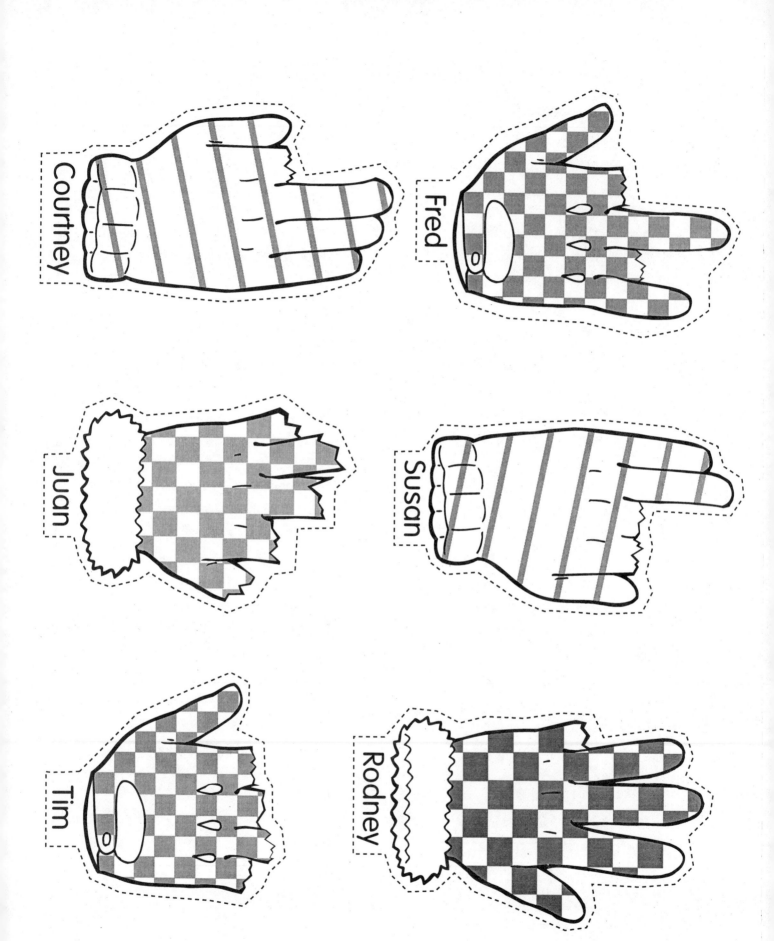

Courtney

Fred

Juan

Susan

Tim

Rodney

Hands-On Thinking Activities

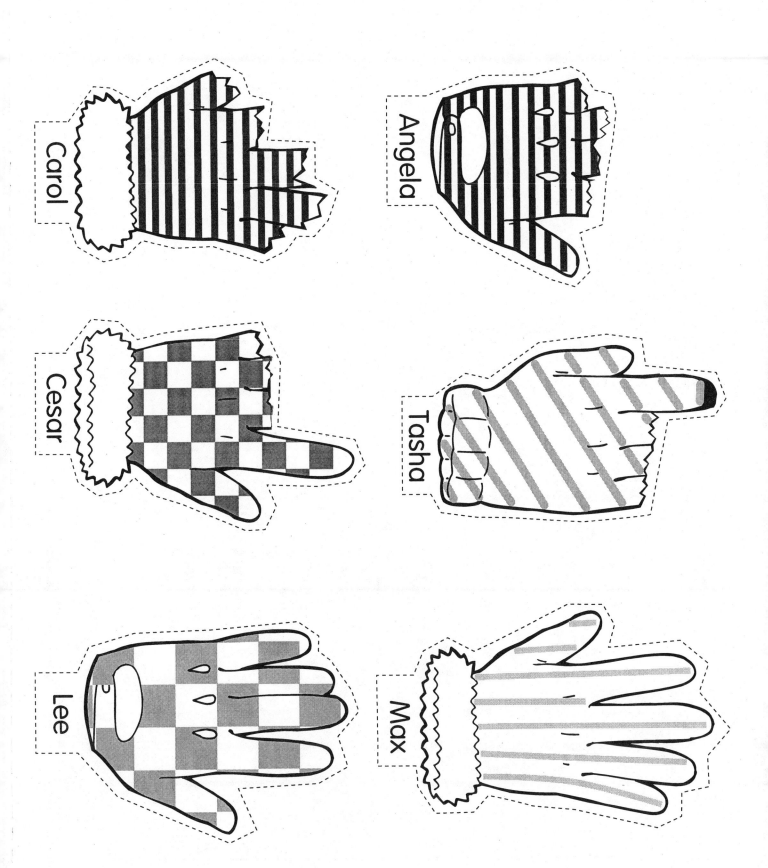

Carol

Angela

Cesar

Tasha

Lee

Max

Hands-On Thinking Activities

Note: Reproduce this sign to place on the table to identify each center.

fold

The Great Glove Game

Thinking Skill - designing
Number of students at this center - *up to 4*
Time required at center - *25 minutes*

Winter Wonder-land

Student Task

Students create a variety of snowflakes by experimenting with folding and cutting paper in different ways.

Materials

- 8 1/2" (22 cm) squares of white copy paper (at least four per student)
- garbage can for scraps
- scissors
- copies of the student record sheet on page 82
- center sign on page 83

Teacher Notes

1. Every snowflake in nature is different. There are also many ways to create interesting paper snowflakes. This activity gives students the opportunity to experiment with some of these techniques. Students may fold paper into squares or diagonals, they may fold the paper twice or many times, they may make simple or complicated cuts. It is an activity that promotes creative thinking by asking students to experiment with different folds and cuts.

2. Most snowflakes in nature are hexagonal. Can students find a way to achieve that shape? What are the best cutting techniques to use to achieve intricate and interesting designs?

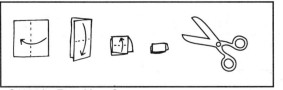

Winter Wonderland

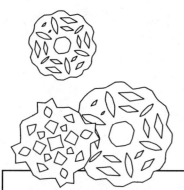

All snowflakes are different. Most snowflakes are hexagonal in shape. Design snowflakes by folding your paper and cutting out small designs on the fold. The more folds and the more small cuts you make the more complicated your design will be.

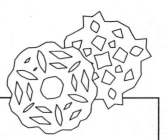

Snowflake ONE:

Number of folds _____ creates _____ sections on your paper.

My snowflake has _____ sides.

Snowflake TWO:

Number of folds _____ creates _____ sections on your paper.

My snowflake has _____ sides.

Snowflake THREE:

Number of folds _____ creates _____ sections on your paper.

My snowflake has _____ sides.

Final Challenge

Design a six-sided snowflake from a square piece of paper.
Use the fewest number of folds to achieve this challenge.
Explain how you did it.

_____

_____

_____

Note: Reproduce this sign to place on the table to identify each center.

fold

Winter Wonder-land

Hands-On Thinking Activities

Spring Activities

	Following Directions	Predicting	Estimating	Interpreting	Sorting	Classifying	Organizing	Designing
Ears to You				✿	✿			
Fruit Frenzy		✿	✿		✿		✿	
Dazzling Daisies				✿	✿		✿	
Fancy Feathers					✿	✿		
Rabbit Round-up	✿			✿				
Crazy Kites					✿	✿	✿	
Lima Bean Bingo							✿	✿
Eggstravagant Eggs			✿	✿				
The Seed Sorter				✿	✿	✿	✿	
Bubble Mania	✿	✿					✿	

Hand-On Thinking Activities

Note: Provide this reproducible for any students who finish a center early.

Name It	a flower	something you can buy in a store	something to eat or drink	a describing word	a boy's name
EXAMPLE: l	lily	lock	lemonade	lumpy	Larry
S					
P					
R					
I					
N					
G					

Hand-On Thinking Activities

Thinking Skills - sorting, interpreting
Number of students at this center - up to 4
Time required at center - 25 minutes

Student Task

Students shake plastic eggs and match pairs based on the sound they hear.

Materials

- 24 plastic eggs filled with:

  (each set of two eggs must contain the same thing)

pennies	small jelly beans
chocolate eggs	marshmallows
rice	safety pins
sunflower seeds	raisins
marbles	dice
thumb tacks	toothpicks

- a basket or container for the filled eggs
- white glue and tape
- copies of the student record sheet on page 87
- center sign on page 88

Teacher Notes

1. Fill each egg with just a few objects (so you can hear them rattle inside) and glue them tightly shut. When the glue is dry, tape the seam securely. A class of 30 students puts a real strain on the eggs. This will keep the eggs shut for good! You may vary contents of the eggs to suit your fancy; however, the student record sheet must reflect what you put in your eggs.

2. Number each egg from 1 to 24 with a permanent pen. Make sure to keep an answer key so YOU will know which eggs contain which objects. You may add excitement to the center by having "prize" eggs to give to people successfully making all of the matches.

3. Students are to shake the eggs, listening carefully to the sound made by the objects inside. When they feel they have made a match, they are to write the numbers on their record sheets.

Ears to You

Get your ears sharpened for this event. The 24 eggs in this basket are filled with objects on the list below. Your job, if you should decide to accept it, is to find two matching eggs with the same objects in them. Identify the eggs by writing their numbers next to the item below you think is in both eggs.

Objects	Egg Numbers
pennies	_____
jelly beans	_____
chocolate eggs	_____
marshmallows	_____
rice	_____
safety pins	_____
sunflower seeds	_____
raisins	_____
marbles	_____
dice	_____
thumb tacks	_____
toothpicks	_____

Hand-On Thinking Activities

Note: Reproduce this sign to place on the table to identify each center.

fold

Ears to You

Thinking Skills - predicting, estimating, sorting, organizing
Number of students at this center - up to 4
Time required at center - 25 minutes

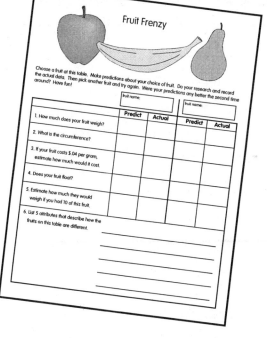

Fruit Frenzy

Student Task
Students make predictions about certain attributes of the fruit at their center.

Materials
- a variety of seasonal fruits (at least eight)
- a balance scale and gram masses
- a ball of string
- scissors
- metric rulers
- a bucket of water
- paper towels
- calculators (optional)
- copies of the student record sheet on page 90
- center sign on page 91

Teacher Notes
1. Students will share the balance scale, string, and bucket of water as they make predictions about the weight, circumference, and ability to float of the fruit. Predictions are recorded on the record sheets, then students research to find how close they came.

2. Make sure children know what "attributes" are before beginning this activity. Instruct students to predict each result **before** the measurements are taken. This ensures higher level thinking skills.

For the Whiz Kid
A third fruit can be measured with results recorded on the back of the record sheet.
A student can show another child his/her findings and have that second student identify the correct fruit.

Fruit Frenzy

Choose a fruit at this table. Make predictions about your choice of fruit. Do your research and record the actual data. Then pick another fruit and try again. Were your predictions any better the second time around? Have fun!

fruit name: _____   fruit name: _____

	Predict	Actual	Predict	Actual
1. How much does your fruit weigh?				
2. What is the circumference?				
3. If your fruit costs $.04 per gram, estimate how much would it cost.				
4. Does your fruit float?				
5. Estimate how much they would weigh if you had 10 of this fruit.				

6. List five attributes that describe how the fruits on this table are different.

_____

_____

_____

_____

_____

Note: Reproduce this sign to place on the table to identify each center.

fold

Thinking Skills - *sorting, interpreting, organizing*
Number of students at this center - *up to 4*
Time required at center - *25 minutes*

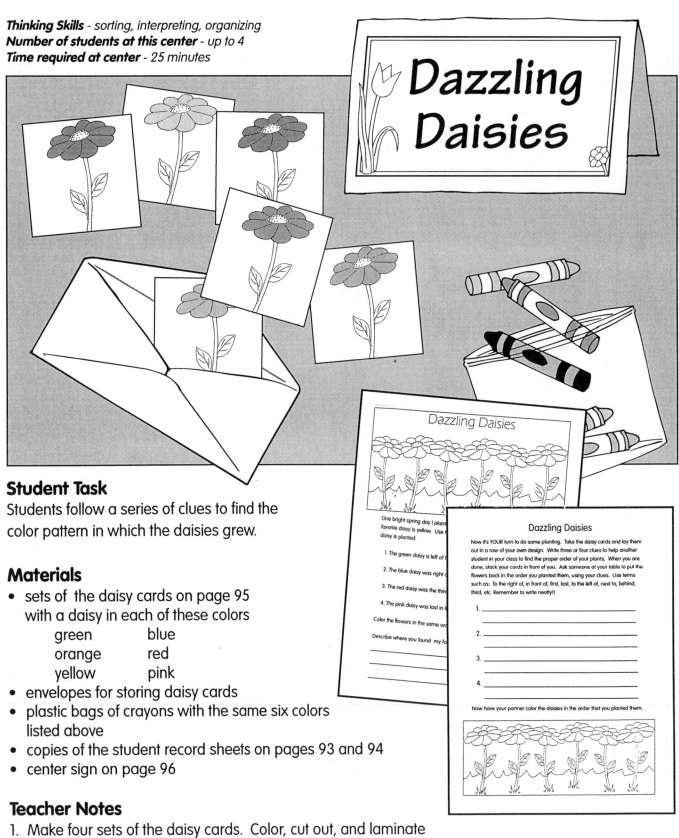

Student Task

Students follow a series of clues to find the color pattern in which the daisies grew.

Materials

- sets of the daisy cards on page 95 with a daisy in each of these colors

green	blue
orange	red
yellow	pink

- envelopes for storing daisy cards
- plastic bags of crayons with the same six colors listed above
- copies of the student record sheets on pages 93 and 94
- center sign on page 96

Teacher Notes

1. Make four sets of the daisy cards. Color, cut out, and laminate the cards. Store each set in an envelope. Students must replace the cards in their own envelope after finishing the activity.

2. Extend the activity by having students develop their own daisy garden puzzle using the form on page 94.

Dazzling Daisies

One bright spring day I planted rows of colorful flowers in my garden. My favorite daisy is yellow. Use the clues below to find out where my favorite daisy is planted.

1. The green daisy is left of the orange daisy and right of the yellow one.

2. The blue daisy is right of the green and left of the orange daisy.

3. The red daisy is the third plant from the left.

4. The pink daisy is last in line on the far right.

Color the flowers in the same order that I planted them.

Describe where you found my favorite color.

_____

_____

_____

Dazzling Daisies

Now it's YOUR turn to do some planting. Take the daisy cards and lay them out in a row of your own design. Write three or four clues to help another student in your class to find the proper order of your plants. When you are done, stack your cards in front of you. Ask someone at your table to put the flowers back in the order you planted them, using your clues. Use terms such as: to the right of, in front of, first, last, to the left of, next to, behind, third, etc. Remember to write neatly!

1. _____

_____

2. _____

_____

3. _____

_____

4. _____

_____

Now have your partner color the daisies in the order that you planted them.

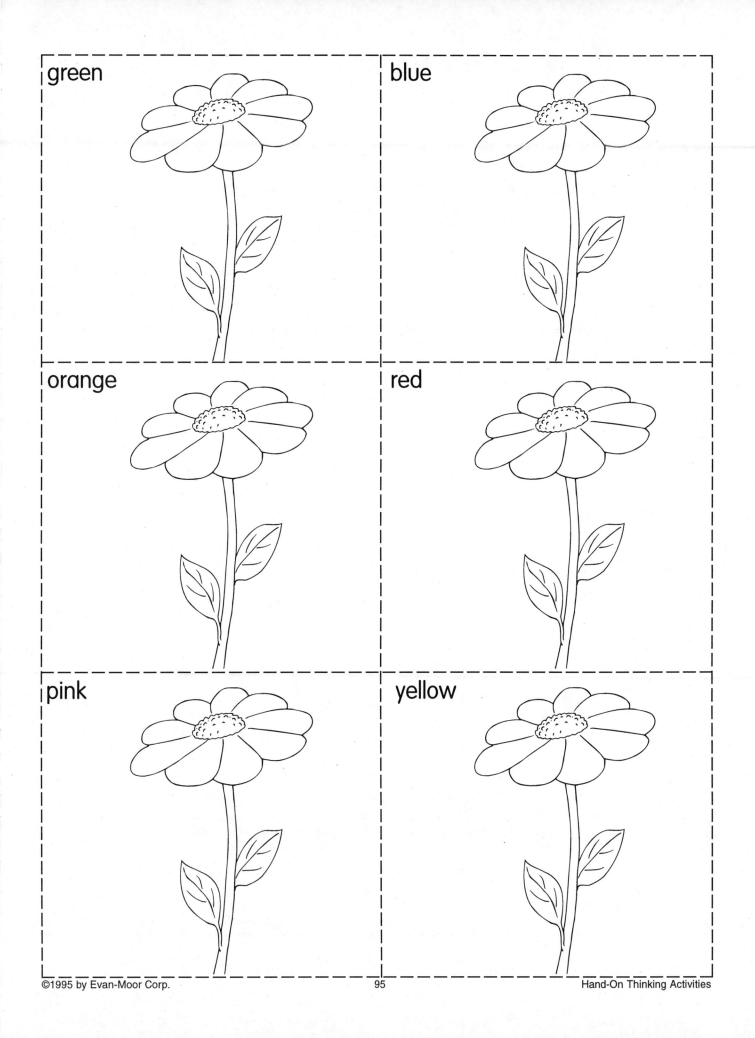

green

blue

orange

red

pink

yellow

Hand-On Thinking Activities

Note: Reproduce this sign to place on the table to identify each center.

fold

Dazzling Daisies

Thinking Skills *- sorting, classifying*
Number of students at this center *- up to 4*
Time required at center *- 25 minutes*

Fancy Feathers

You'll feel light as a feather when you're done with this! Take your bag, dump it out, and take a good look. How are all these feathers alike and how are they different? Pick ONE attribute for your first try. If you picked size, you would put the feathers into groups such as: small, medium, large, extra large. Be even more creative and come up with **another way** to classify them. Remember, pick ONE characteristic, then put them into groups. Record your data below.

First try:

ATTRIBUTE: _____

Group 1	Group 2	Group 3	Group 4

Second try:

ATTRIBUTE: _____

Group 1	Group 2	Group 3	Group 4

Student Task

Students organize feathers into sets according to similar attributes.

Materials

- plastic bags
- assorted feathers
  (check hobby or craft stores)
- copies of the student record sheet on page 98
- center sign on page 99

Teacher Notes

1. Each baggie should contain at least ten feathers which can be grouped in a variety of ways (size, color, design, texture, etc.).

2. Make sure students understand what an ATTRIBUTE is as you are giving directions to the group about the center. Encourage students to make unusual groupings. There are places to record four separate groupings on the student record sheet. Students use as many places as they need.

3. Students are to repeat the activity using a different attribute.

                                       Hand-On Thinking Activities

Fancy Feathers

You'll feel light as a feather when you're done with this! Take your bag, dump it out, and take a good look. How are all these feathers alike and how are they different? Pick ONE attribute for your first try. If you picked size, you would put the feathers into groups such as: small, medium, large, extra large. Be even more creative and come up with **another way** to classify them. Remember, pick ONE characteristic, then put them into groups. Record your data below.

First try:

ATTRIBUTE: _____

Group 1	Group 2	Group 3	Group 4

Second try:

ATTRIBUTE: _____

Group 1	Group 2	Group 3	Group 4

Note: Reproduce this sign to place on the table to identify each center.

fold

Thinking Skills - *interpreting, following directions*
Number of students at this center - *up to 2*
Time required at center - *25 minutes*

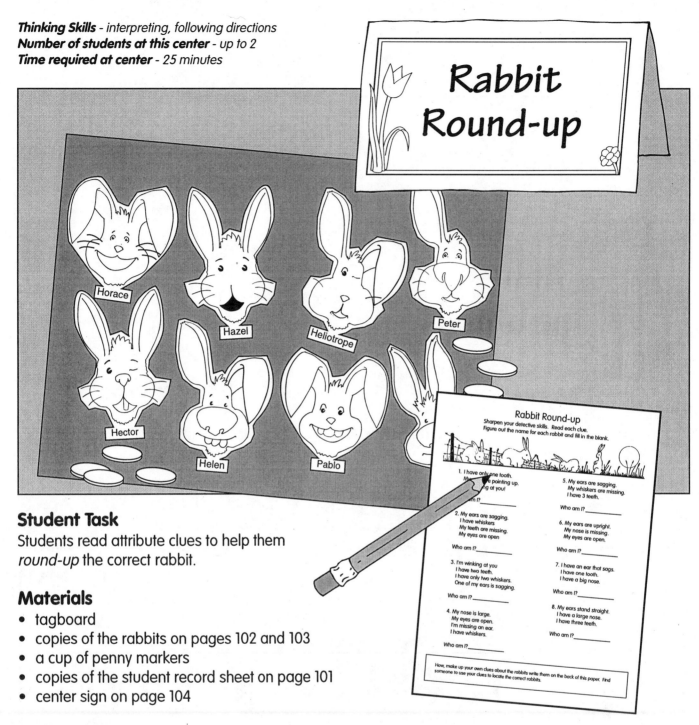

Rabbit Round-up

Student Task

Students read attribute clues to help them *round-up* the correct rabbit.

Materials

- tagboard
- copies of the rabbits on pages 102 and 103
- a cup of penny markers
- copies of the student record sheet on page 101
- center sign on page 104

Teacher Notes

1. Prepare a chart with the rabbits on pages 102 and 103. Glue them on a sheet of colored tagboard and laminate. Place the chart on the center work table.

2. Students are to use the clues on their record sheet to help them locate the correct rabbit being described each time. Students can use the markers to select the rabbits that fit the group of clues being studied. As rabbits are eliminated, the markers are removed. The rabbit with the one remaining marker should be the correct answer.

3. When students have completed their worksheet, have them turn their papers over and make up their own clues to challenge classmates.

©1995 by Evan-Moor Corp.   100   Hand-On Thinking Activities

Rabbit Round-up

Sharpen your detective skills. Read each clue.
Figure out the name for each rabbit and fill in the blank.

1. I have only one tooth.
   My ears are pointing up.
   I'm winking at you!

   Who am I?_____

2. My ears are sagging.
   I have whiskers.
   My teeth are missing.
   My eyes are open.

   Who am I?_____

3. I'm winking at you.
   I have two teeth.
   I have only two whiskers.
   One of my ears is sagging.

   Who am I?_____

4. My nose is large.
   My eyes are open.
   I'm missing an ear.
   I have whiskers.

   Who am I?_____

5. My ears are sagging.
   My whiskers are missing.
   I have three teeth.

   Who am I?_____

6. My ears are upright.
   My nose is missing.
   My eyes are open.

   Who am I?_____

7. I have an ear that sags.
   I have one tooth.
   I have a big nose.

   Who am I?_____

8. My ears stand straight.
   I have a large nose.
   I have three teeth.

   Who am I?_____

Now, make up your own clues about the rabbits and write them on the back of this paper.
Find someone to use your clues to locate the correct rabbits.

Hand-On Thinking Activities

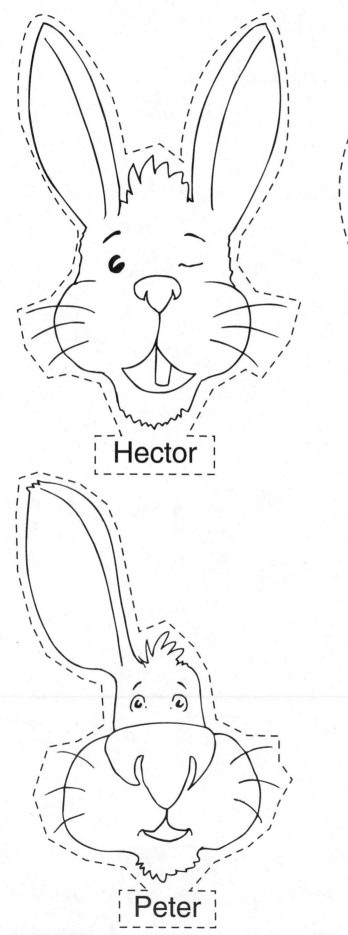

Hector

Pablo

Peter

Ann

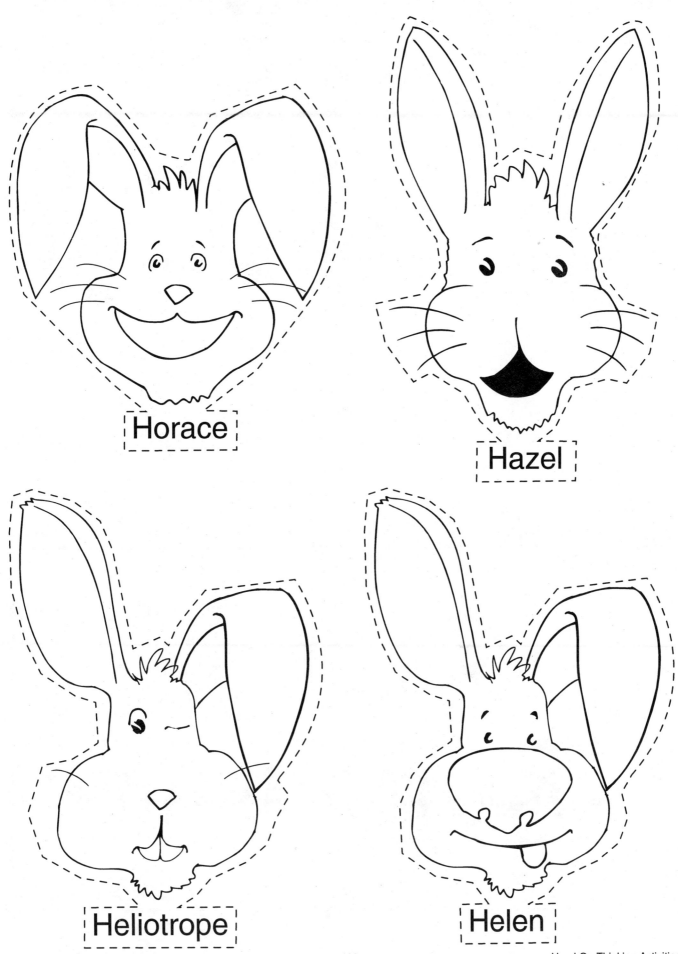

Horace

Hazel

Heliotrope

Helen

Hand-On Thinking Activities

Note: Reproduce this sign to place on the table to identify each center.

fold

Thinking Skills *- sorting, classifying, organizing*
Number of students at this center *- up to 4*
Time required at center *- 25 minutes*

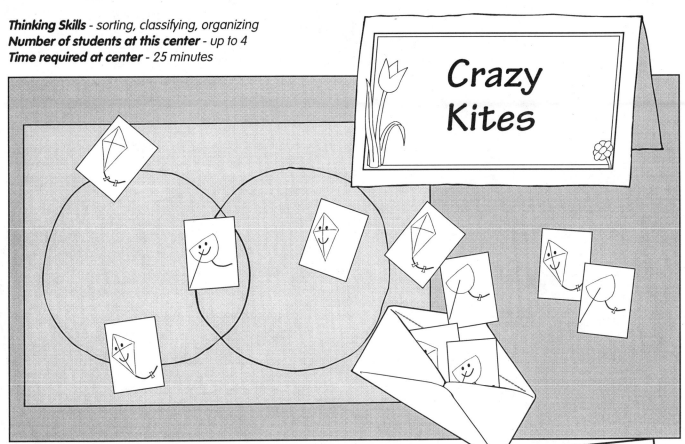

Crazy Kites

Student Task

Students sort kites by attributes using a Venn diagram.

Materials

- plastic bags
- small kites on page 107 colored and pasted on construction paper
- four 12" x 18" (30.5 X 45.7 cm) sheets of construction paper each containing a large Venn diagram
- copies of the student record sheet on page 106
- center sign on page 107

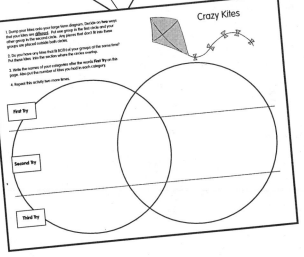

Teacher Notes

1. Prepare the sets of kites and the Venn diagram work mats. Place a set of kites in each plastic bag.

2. Be sure your students understand the term *attributes* (a certain quality or characteristic of an object, such as color, shape, size, etc.) and how a Venn diagram works before they begin.

3. Children will separate their kites by attributes and list the results on their record sheet. They will be sorting kites into three groups: two groups with distinctly separate attributes and one group that combines attributes of the other two. For example:

5. Students are to repeat this activity three times and record the results.

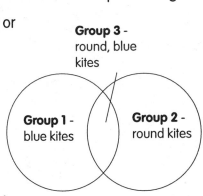

Group 3 - round, blue kites

Group 1 - blue kites

Group 2 - round kites

Crazy Kites

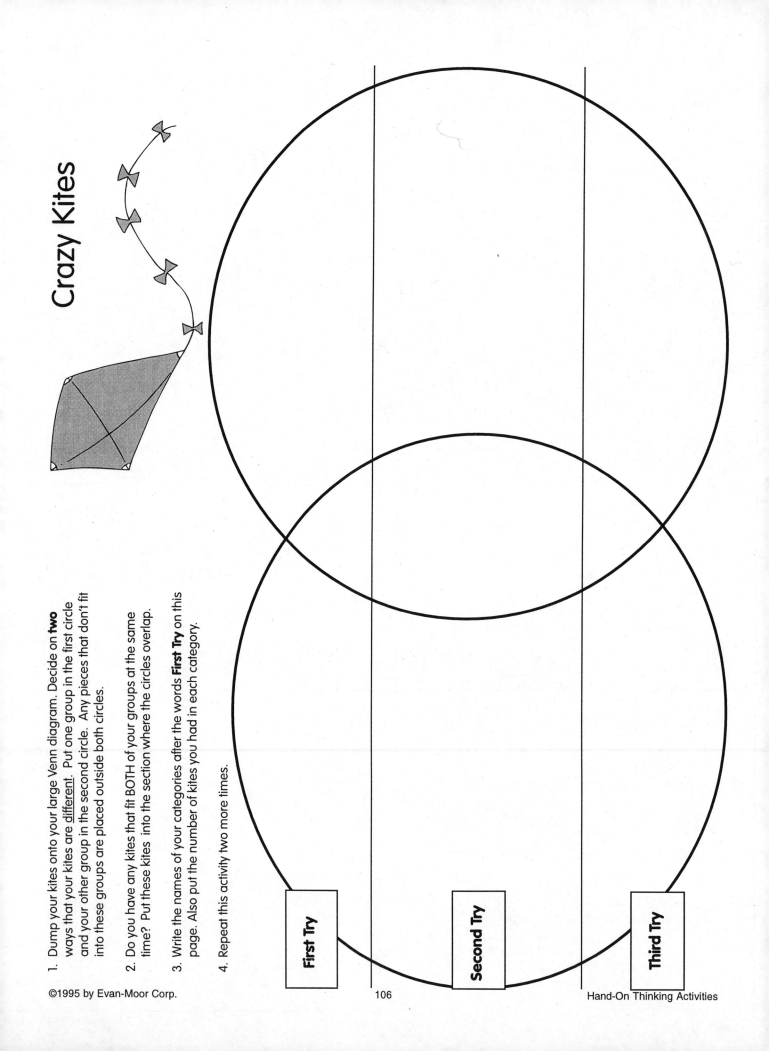

1. Dump your kites onto your large Venn diagram. Decide on **two** ways that your kites are <u>different</u>. Put one group in the first circle and your other group in the second circle. Any pieces that don't fit into these groups are placed outside both circles.

2. Do you have any kites that fit BOTH of your groups at the same time? Write the names of your categories after the words **First Try** on this page. Also put the number of kites you had in each category.

3. Write the names of your categories after the words **First Try** on this page. Also put the number of kites you had in each category.

4. Repeat this activity two more times.

First Try

Second Try

Third Try

Hand-On Thinking Activities

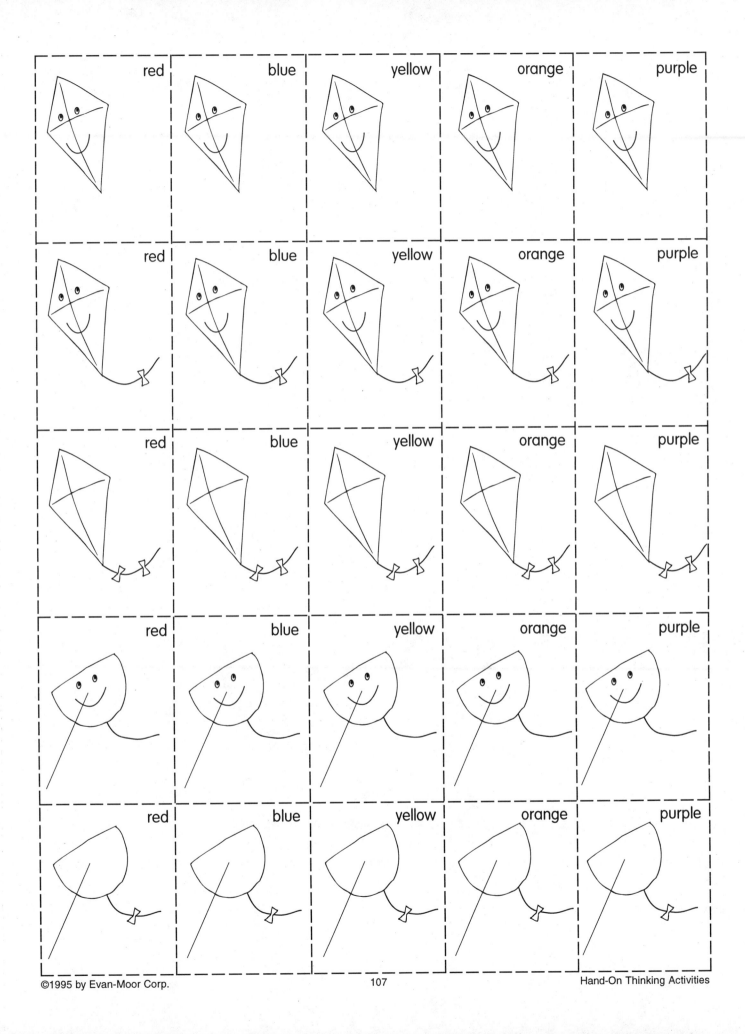

red   blue   yellow   orange   purple

Hand-On Thinking Activities

Note: Reproduce this sign to place on the table to identify each center.

fold

Crazy Kites

Thinking Skills - *organizing, designing*
Number of students at this center - *up to 4*
Time required at center - *25 minutes*

Lima Bean Bingo

1. Use four beans from the cup.

2. Place each bean in a square. Make sure there is only one bean in each column down and each row across.

3. Record your pattern below. Then try again. See how many ways you can solve this puzzle.

1	2	3	4
5	6	7	8
9	10	11	12
13	14	15	16

Where are the beans?

First try: _____

Second try: _____

Third try: _____

Fourth try: _____

Fifth try: _____

Sixth try: _____

Student Task

Students create patterns on a grid using lima beans.

Materials

- a container of large lima beans
- copies of the student record sheet on page 110
- center sign on page 111

Teacher Notes

1. Have students take four lima beans from the container and keep them.

2. Students are to find at least six patterns using the grid on their student record sheets. There are many solutions to this puzzle. Students can work on finding them as long as time permits. Have students put these solutions on the back of their student record sheet.

Lima Bean Bingo

1. Use four beans from the cup.

2. Place each bean in a square. Make sure there is only one bean in each column down and each row across.

3. Record your pattern below. Then try again. See how many ways you can solve this puzzle.

1	2	3	4
5	6	7	8
9	10	11	12
13	14	15	16

Where are the beans?

First try: _____ _____ _____ _____

Second try: _____ _____ _____ _____

Third try: _____ _____ _____ _____

Fourth try: _____ _____ _____ _____

Fifth try: _____ _____ _____ _____

Sixth try: _____ _____ _____ _____

Note: Reproduce this sign to place on the table to identify each center.

fold

Lima Bean
Bingo

Thinking Skills - *estimating, interpreting*
Number of students at this center - *up to 4*
Time required at center - *25 minutes*

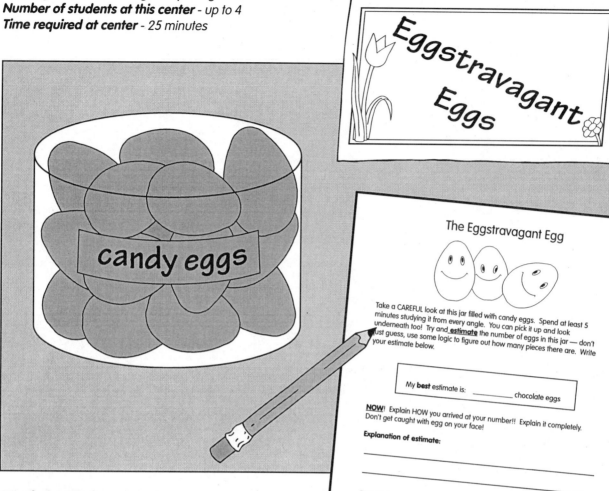

The Eggstravagant Egg

Take a CAREFUL look at this jar filled with candy eggs. Spend at least 5 minutes studying it from every angle. You can pick it up and look underneath too! Try and **estimate** the number of eggs in this jar — don't just guess, use some logic to figure out how many pieces there are. Write your estimate below.

My **best** estimate is: _____ chocolate eggs

NOW! Explain HOW you arrived at your number!! Explain it completely. Don't get caught with egg on your face!

Explanation of estimate:

_____
_____
_____
_____
_____
_____
_____
_____

Student Task

Students estimate the number of small chocolate eggs in the jar. Then they are to write a complete explanation of how they arrived at their estimation. The teacher chooses the three closest estimations and reads them to the class. The class votes on the clearest explanation.

Materials

- a jar of small foil-wrapped chocolate eggs
- student record sheet on page 113
- center sign on page 114

Teacher Notes

1. Make sure students understand that a complete explanation must be logical, thorough and sequential.

2. The teacher needs to decide ahead of time if the jar of chocolate eggs will be given as a prize to the person who writes the best explanation.

Eggstravagant Eggs

Take a CAREFUL look at this jar filled with candy eggs. Spend at least five minutes studying it from every angle. You can pick it up and look underneath, too! Try and **estimate** the number of eggs in this jar — don't just guess, use some logic to figure out how many pieces there are. Write your estimate below.

My **best** estimate is: _____ chocolate eggs

NOW! Explain HOW you arrived at your number! Explain it completely. Don't get caught with egg on your face!

Explanation of estimate:

_____

_____

_____

_____

_____

_____

Note: Reproduce this sign to place on the table to identify each center.

fold

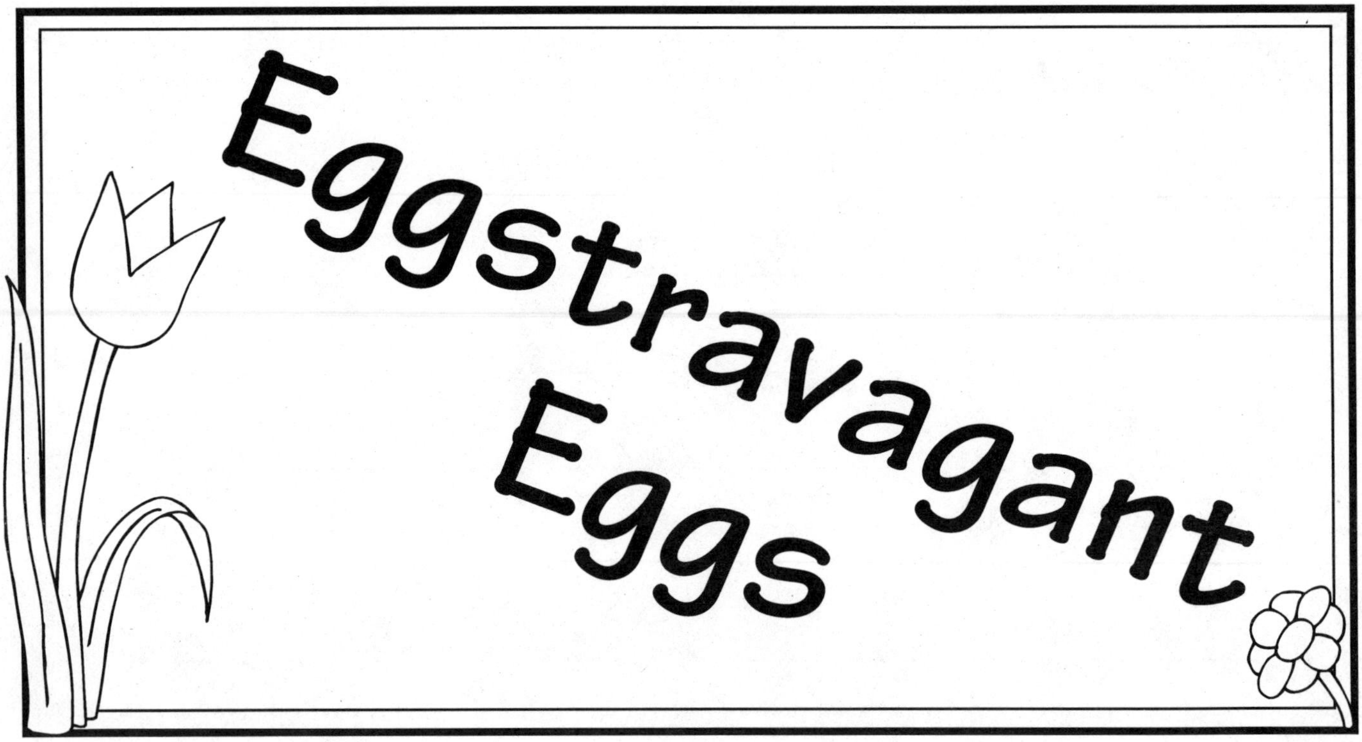

Eggstravagant Eggs

Thinking Skills - *interpreting, sorting, classifying, organizing*
Number of students at this center - *up to 4*
Time required at center - *25 minutes*

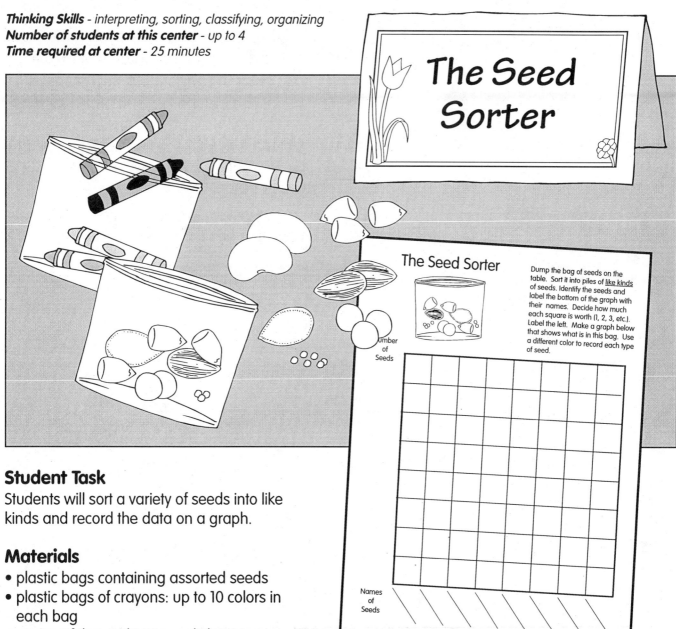

The Seed Sorter

Dump the bag of seeds on the table. Sort it into piles of <u>like kinds</u> of seeds. Identify the seeds and label the bottom of the graph with their names. Decide how much each square is worth (1, 2, 3, etc.). Label the left. Make a graph below that shows what is in this bag. Use a different color to record each type of seed.

Number of Seeds

Names of Seeds

Student Task

Students will sort a variety of seeds into like kinds and record the data on a graph.

Materials

- plastic bags containing assorted seeds
- plastic bags of crayons: up to 10 colors in each bag
- copies of the student record sheet on page 116
- center sign on page 117

Teacher Notes

1. Prepare the plastic bags of seeds being sure to use bigger seeds that are easily handled. You should have up to 10 varieties of seeds, with a different number of each kind, in each bag to make an interesting graph.

2. As you explain this center to the class, be sure to identify the types of seeds you are using. You may want to put up a chart with each type of seed and its name as a reference for your students.

3. Students sort their seeds, count them, and record the data on their graphs.

For the Whiz Kid

Have these students list several observations that can be learned from the final graph on the back of their record sheet.

The Seed Sorter

Dump the bag of seeds on the table. Sort them into piles of <u>like kinds</u> of seeds. Identify the seeds and label the bottom of the graph with their names. Decide how much each square is worth (1, 2, 3, etc.). Label the left. Make a graph below that shows what is in this bag. Use a different color to record each type of seed.

Number
of
Seeds

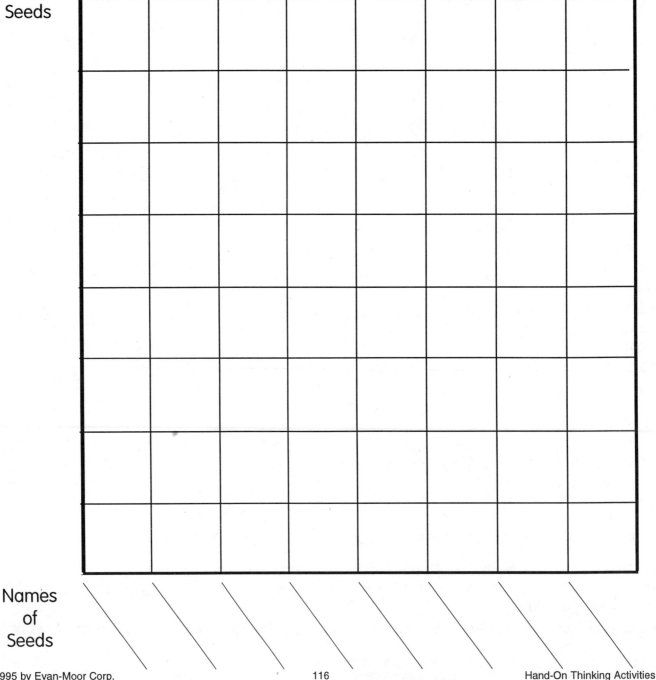

Names
of
Seeds

Note: Reproduce this sign to place on the table to identify each center.

fold

The Seed Sorter

 Hand-On Thinking Activities

Thinking Skills - *predicting, organizing, following directions*
Number of students at this center - *up to 4*
Time required at center - *25 minutes*

Student Task
Students measure the diameter of the bubbles they blow.

Materials
- a quart of bubble solution
- a straw for each student
- a metric or standard ruler
- a large roll of hand towels
- sponges
- garbage can for wet towels
- copies of the student record sheet on page 119
- center sign on page 120

Soap Mixture
1 quart (1 liter) of water and 1/2 cup (125 ml) of soap. Try making a bubble. If it breaks too fast, add a bit more liquid dish soap. Ivory makes a stronger bubble than other brands.

Teacher Notes
1. A volunteer is needed in this center to keep the students on task and keep them rotating through the center in a timely manner. Once students get to this center, they tend to stay forever.

2. Use a plastic ruler to scrape the soapy water off the table into an empty garbage can. The floor around the rim of the table will get wet. Just get used to that fact and have plenty of paper towels handy.

3. Students will be working to determine the diameter of the bubbles they create. Be sure they understand the directions on the student record sheet before they begin the activity.

For the Whiz Kid
Have them attempt to make a bubble INSIDE another bubble on the table and to work with another student to make ONE BIG bubble.

Bubble Mania

How are your bubble making skills?
At this center you will test your patience and lung control.

1. Place a small amount of bubble mixture in front of you on the wet table. Using a NEW straw, just touch the layer of soap and blow slowly and gently. Make the biggest bubble you can.
2. When the bubble breaks, quickly use a ruler to measure the diameter of the soapy ring left on the table.
3. Record your results below.
4. Repeat the activity several times.

Bubble Diameter

Trial 1 _____

Trial 2 _____

Trial 3 _____

Trial 4 _____

diameter

What do you think helps to make a BIG bubble?
List three variables below.

1. _____

2. _____

3. _____

Note: Reproduce this sign to place on the table to identify each center.

fold

Bubble Mania

Summer Activities

	Following Directions	Predicting	Estimating	Interpreting	Sorting	Classifying	Organizing	Designing
A Farmer in the Dell	⛵							
Blowing in the Wind				⛵				
Vehicular Vacations				⛵			⛵	
Hot Shots		⛵		⛵				
Gooey Gumballs			⛵	⛵				
Mouth-watering Watermelons				⛵				
Flying High				⛵			⛵	
Frozen Fun	⛵							
Summer Sleuthing				⛵			⛵	⛵
Seedy Characters			⛵	⛵				

Hand-On Thinking Activities

Name It	cloth or clothing	a city or country	an objectin space	a food or drink	a naming word (noun)
EXAMPLE: **P**	pinafore	Paris	planet	peanut butter	pony
S					
U					
M					
M					
E					
R					

Hand-On Thinking Activities

Thinking Skill - following directions
Number of students at this center - up to 4
Time required at center - 25 minutes

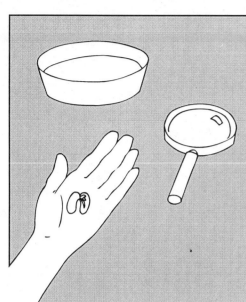

Student Task

Students observe and label the parts of a soaked bean seed. Then they will plant bean seeds for future observations.

Materials

For every student:
- a large lima bean (soak overnight)
- a dry lima bean seed
- an empty school milk carton
- about a 1/2 cup (125 ml) of soil
- student record sheet on page 124

General materials:
- magnifying glasses
- water and spoons for watering
- skinny nails for poking drainage holes in the carton
- newspaper to cover the table
- masking tape and permanent marker for labeling milk cartons
- center sign on page 125

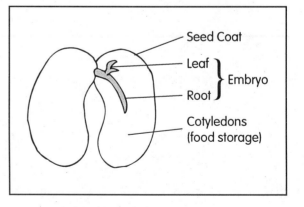

Teacher Notes

1. Prepare a chart of the diagram of the inside of a seed. Place it in the center for student reference.

2. Seeds intended for gardening will germinate more successfully than dried beans from the grocery store.

3. Students follow the directions on their record sheet. They examine the soaked lima bean and label the parts.

A Farmer in the Dell

Take a look.

It's time to be a scientist! Take out one lima bean that is soaking in water. Pull off the outer layer, and split the bean in half with your fingernail. Use the magnifying glass to observe the inside of the bean seed. Make a diagram of what you see. Label the parts:

        root

        leaf

        seed coat

        embryo

        cotyledons

Now it's your turn to be the farmer.

☐ 1. Take an empty milk carton, poke a few holes in the bottom with the nail at your table.

☐ 2. Fill the carton with soil.

☐ 3. Make a hole in the soil with your finger. Place an unsoaked seed in the hole, and cover it with soil. Pat the soil lightly.

☐ 4. Use a spoon to water the plant. The plant should be damp, not soaking wet.

☐ 5. Label your carton with your name, the kind of seed you planted, and the date.

☐ 6. Keep the milk carton in a sunny window and water when the soil dries out.

☐ 7. When the plant is 2 inches (5 centimeters) tall, transplant it in your garden. Keep track of the growth of your plant over the summer. Good eating!

Hand-On Thinking Activities

Note: Reproduce this sign to place on the table to identify each center.

fold

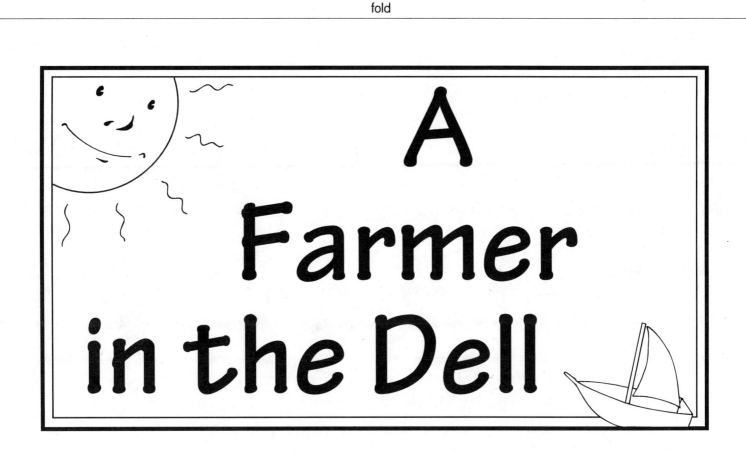

Thinking Skill - *interpreting*
Number of students at this center - *up to 4*
Time required at center - *25 minutes*

Student Task

Students blow bubbles and then observe what happens when they create an air current above the bubble with a cardboard fan.

Materials

- bubble mixture:
    - 1 gallon (4 liters) of water mixed with
    - 1 cup (250 ml) of liquid dish detergent (Ivory is best)
    - 1/8 cup (30 ml) glycerin (optional)
- a sturdy paper cup for each child
  (with the bottom cut out)
- 4" x 8" (10 X 20.5 cm) pieces of sturdy cardboard
- plastic bowls
- copies of the student record sheet on page 127
- center sign on page 128

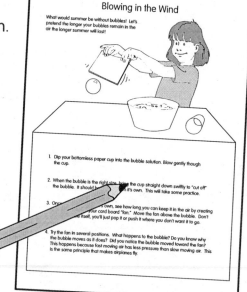

Teacher Notes

1. This center is best done in an open space where you have plenty of room.

2. A parent volunteer is helpful in this center. Be sure the volunteer is prepared to demonstrate the activity.

3. Demonstrate for students how to release the bubble from their paper cup. Bring the cup straight down with a swift motion to release the bubble and set it in motion.

4. You will also need to demonstrate how to fan the bubble with the cardboard.

Blowing in the Wind

What would summer be without bubbles! Let's pretend the longer your bubbles remain in the air the longer summer will last!

1. Dip your bottomless paper cup into the bubble solution. Blow gently though the cup.

2. When the bubble is the right size, bring the cup straight down swiftly to "cut off" the bubble. It should begin to float on its own. This will take some practice.

3. Once your bubble is on its own, see how long you can keep it in the air by creating an air current with your cardboard "fan." Move the fan above the bubble. Don't fan the bubble itself, you'll just pop it or push it where you don't want it to go.

4. Try the fan in several positions. What happens to the bubble? Do you know why the bubble moves as it does? Did you notice the bubble moved toward the fan? This happens because fast-moving air has less pressure than slow-moving air. This is the same principle that makes airplanes fly.

Hand-On Thinking Activities

Note: Reproduce this sign to place on the table to identify each center.

fold

Blowing in the Wind

Thinking Skills - *interpreting, organizing*
Number of students at this center - *up to 2*
Time required at center - *25 minutes*

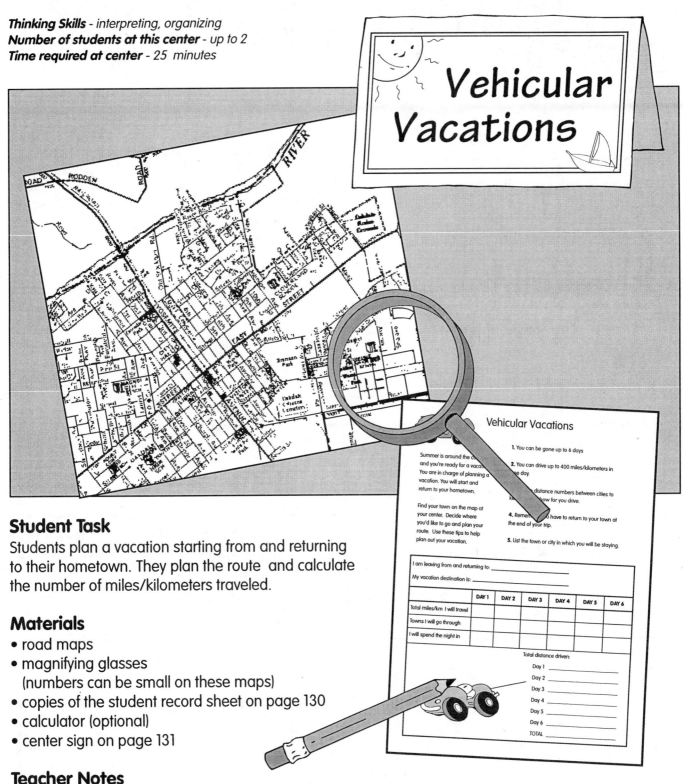

Vehicular Vacations

Summer is around the c[...]
and you're ready for a vaca[...]
You are in charge of planning a
vacation. You will start and
return to your hometown.

Find your town on the map at
your center. Decide where
you'd like to go and plan your
route. Use these tips to help
plan out your vacation.

1. You can be gone up to 6 days

2. You can drive up to 400 miles/kilometers in
[...]e day.

[...] distance numbers between cities to
[...]ow far you drive.

4. Reme[...] have to return to your town at
the end of your trip.

5. List the town or city in which you will be staying.

I am leaving from and returning to: _____

My vacation destination is: _____

	DAY 1	DAY 2	DAY 3	DAY 4	DAY 5	DAY 6
Total miles/km I will travel						
Towns I will go through						
I will spend the night in						

Total distance driven:

Day 1 _____
Day 2 _____
Day 3 _____
Day 4 _____
Day 5 _____
Day 6 _____
TOTAL _____

Student Task

Students plan a vacation starting from and returning to their hometown. They plan the route and calculate the number of miles/kilometers traveled.

Materials

- road maps
- magnifying glasses
  (numbers can be small on these maps)
- copies of the student record sheet on page 130
- calculator (optional)
- center sign on page 131

Teacher Notes

1. In order to do this activity students must have had experience reading maps and computing distances on them.

2. This activity can be done independently or in pairs with students planning a common vacation.

3. Extend this activity by having students calculate the cost of the gas they would use on this trip. You will need to give them the average distance per gallon/liter and the cost of the gas.

Vehicular Vacations

Summer is around the corner and you're ready for a vacation! You are in charge of planning a vacation. You will start and return to your hometown.

Find your town on the map at your center. Decide where you'd like to go and plan your route. Use these tips to help plan out your vacation.

1. You can be gone up to 6 days.

2. You can drive up to 400 miles/kilometers in one day.

3. Use the distance numbers between cities to keep track of how far you drive.

4. Remember you have to return to your town at the end of your trip.

5. List the towns or cities in which you will be staying.

I am leaving from and returning to: _____

My vacation destination is: _____

	DAY 1	DAY 2	DAY 3	DAY 4	DAY 5	DAY 6
Total miles/km I will travel						
Towns I will go through						
I will spend the night in						

Total distance driven:

Day 1 _____

Day 2 _____

Day 3 _____

Day 4 _____

Day 5 _____

Day 6 _____

TOTAL _____

Note: Reproduce this sign to place on the table to identify each center.

fold

Thinking Skills - *predicting, interpreting*
Number of students at this center - *up to 4*
Time required at center - *25 minutes*

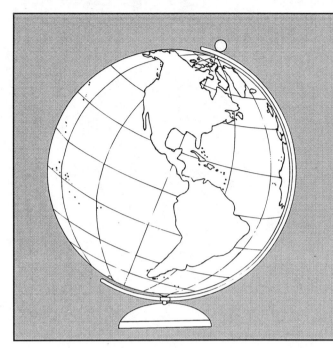

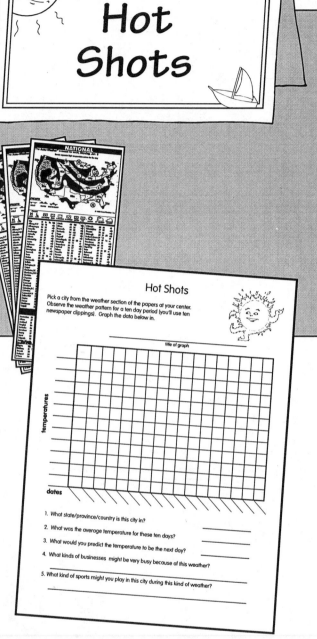

Student Task

Students select a city and keep track of the highest temperature each day for a period of ten days.
Then they graph their findings and interpret the results.

Materials

- sets of:
  10 days of newspaper clippings of the international weather listings
- small world map or globe
- copies of the student record sheet on page 133
- center sign on page 134

Teacher Notes

1. Staple the newspaper clippings together in order.

2. Write in the temperatures in Fahrenheit or Celsius before reproducing page 133.

3. Have students help each other find the location of their cities on the world map or globe. They are to graph the weather data on their record sheet.

4. Students need to know how to find an average temperature in order to complete this activity.

> ***Averaging***: *Add all the data and then divide that answer by how many numbers were used.*

Hot Shots

Pick a city from the weather section of the papers at your center. Observe the weather pattern for a ten-day period (you'll use ten newspaper clippings). Graph the data below.

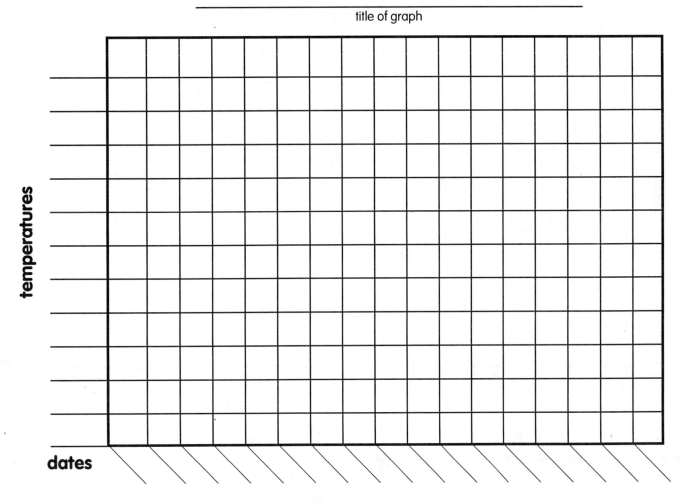

title of graph

temperatures

dates

1. What state/province/country is this city in? _____

2. What was the average temperature for these ten days? _____

3. What would you predict the temperature to be the next day? _____

4. What kinds of businesses might be very busy because of this weather?

_____

5. What kind of sports might you play in this city during this kind of weather?

_____

Hand-On Thinking Activities

Note: Reproduce this sign to place on the table to identify each center.

fold

Hand-On Thinking Activities

Thinking Skills - *estimating, interpreting*
Number of students at this center - *1*
Time required at center - *25 minutes*

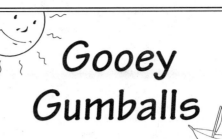

Gooey Gumballs

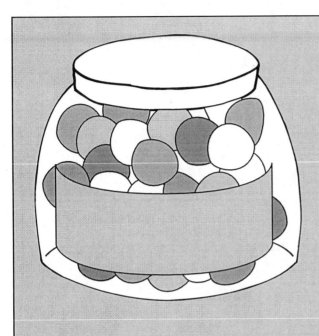

Gooey Gumballs
Part One

Take a careful look at this jar filled with gumballs. Spend at least 5 minutes studying it from every angle. You can pick it up and look underneath too! Try and **estimate** the number 9of hum in this jar--don't guess. Use some logic to figure out how many pieces there are. Write your estimate below.

My best estimate is: _____ gumballs

Explain HOW you arrived at your number. Explain it completely.

Explanation of estimate:

_____
_____
_____
_____
_____
_____
_____
_____
_____

Student Task

Part One

Students estimate the number of gumballs in the jar. Then they are to write a complete explanation on how they arrived at their estimation. The teacher chooses the three closest estimations and reads them to the class. The class votes on the clearest explanation.

Part Two

Students experience further practice in estimation.

Materials

- center sign on page 138
  Part One
- a jar of gumballs
- record sheet on page 136
  Part Two
- 2 empty jars, different sizes
- marbles - enough to fill the largest jar (not more than 100)
- a copy of the student record sheets on pages 137

Teacher Notes

1. Be sure students understand that a "complete" explanation must be logical, thorough, and sequential.

2. The teacher needs to decide ahead of time if the jar of candy will be given as a prize to the person who writes the best explanation.

Gooey Gumballs

Part One

Take a careful look at this jar filled with gumballs. Spend at least five minutes studying it from every angle. You can pick it up and look underneath too! Try and **estimate** the number of gumballs in this jar--don't guess. Use some logic to figure out how many pieces there are. Write your estimate below.

My best estimate is: _____ gumballs

Explain HOW you arrived at your number. Explain it completely.

Explanation of estimate:

_____

_____

_____

_____

_____

_____

_____

_____

Gooey Gumballs
Part Two

Jar 1

Draw the jar here.

Take a close look at empty jar number 1 and the bag of objects next to it. Make an estimate of how many of these objects you think will fit into the jar. Record your estimate below and then fill up the jar, counting the number of objects it takes.

Estimation _____ **Results** _____

Jar 2

Draw the jar here.

Empty jar number 1. Take a look at jar number 2. Knowing what you now know, how many of these objects will it take to fill jar number 2? Record your prediction and then fill up jar number 2. How did you do?

Estimation _____ **Results** _____

Do you want to go back now to your estimation of the Gooey Gumballs Jar and change anything you wrote?

Note: Reproduce this sign to place on the table to identify each center.

fold

Gooey
Gumballs

Hand-On Thinking Activities

Thinking Skill - interpreting
Number of students at this center - up to 2
Time required at center - 25 minutes

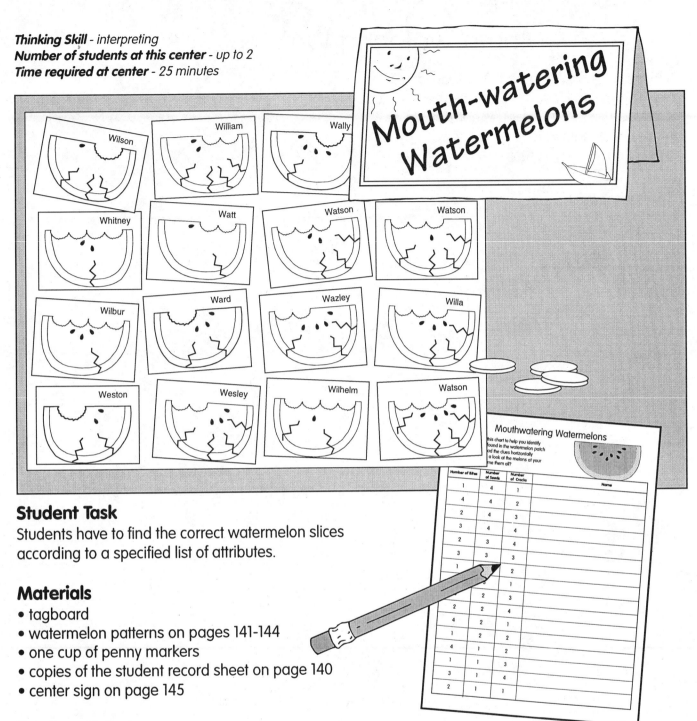

Student Task

Students have to find the correct watermelon slices according to a specified list of attributes.

Materials

- tagboard
- watermelon patterns on pages 141-144
- one cup of penny markers
- copies of the student record sheet on page 140
- center sign on page 145

Teacher Notes

1. A parent volunteer can be a big help in this center as students try to keep track of the different attributes of sixteen watermelon slices.

2. Prepare the *Mouth-watering Watermelon* graphic using the patterns provided. Cut out the individual slices, glue them on a sheet of tagboard, and laminate.

3. Students can use the markers to keep track of the watermelon slices fitting the clues. As the slices are eliminated, the markers are removed. The slice with the one remaining marker should be the correct answer. For example:

> If the first clue says "red," a marker is put on all red slices. If the next clue says "three cracks," the counters will be taken off all red slices that do not have three cracks. This process continues through all of the clues.

Mouth-watering Watermelons

Use the clues on this chart to help you identify the watermelons found in the watermelon patch at your center. Read the clues horizontally (across), then take a look at the melons at your table. Can you name them all?

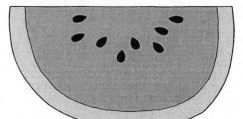

	Number of Bites	Number of Seeds	Number of Cracks	Name
1.	1	4	1	
2.	4	4	2	
3.	2	4	3	
4.	3	4	4	
5.	2	3	4	
6.	3	3	3	
7.	1	3	2	
8.	4	3	1	
9.	3	2	3	
10.	2	2	4	
11.	2	2	3	
12.	1	2	2	
13.	4	1	2	
14.	1	1	3	
15.	3	1	4	
16.	2	1	1	

Hand-On Thinking Activities

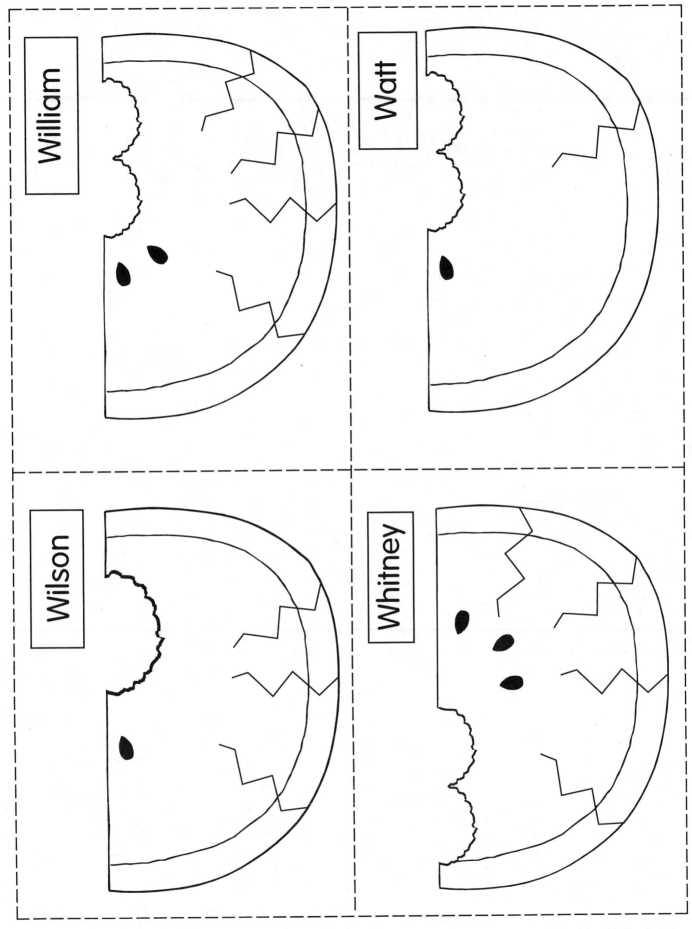

William

Watt

Wilson

Whitney

141

Hand-On Thinking Activities

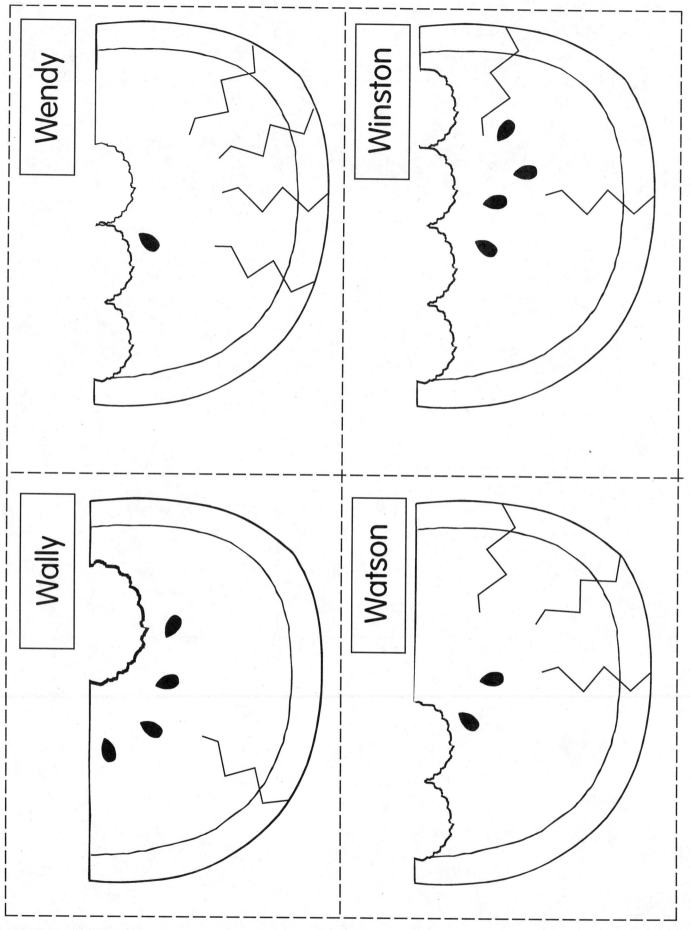

Wendy

Winston

Wally

Watson

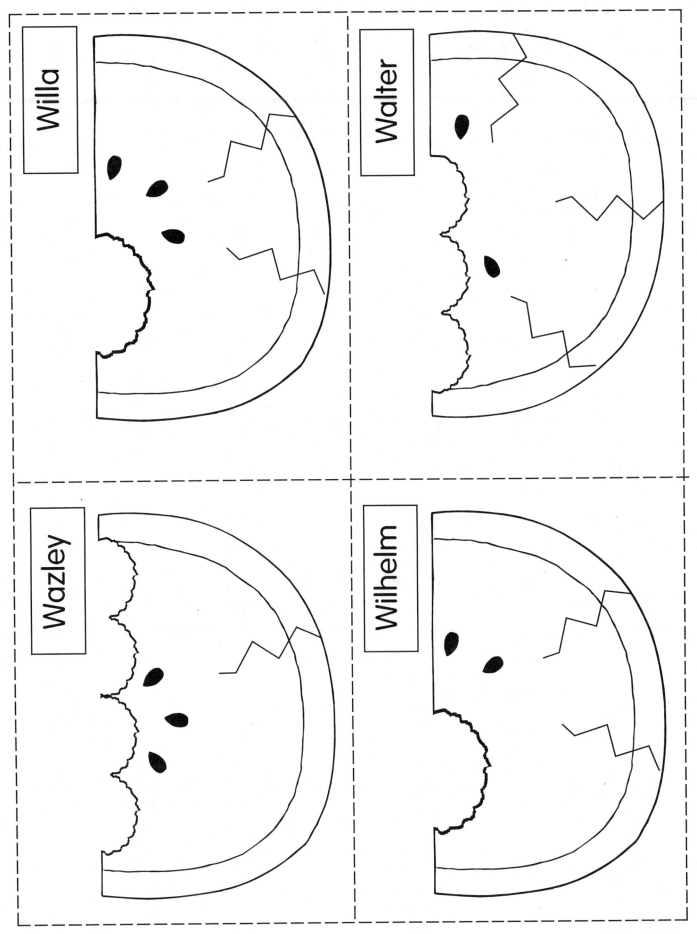

Willa

Walter

Wazley

Wilhelm

Hand-On Thinking Activities

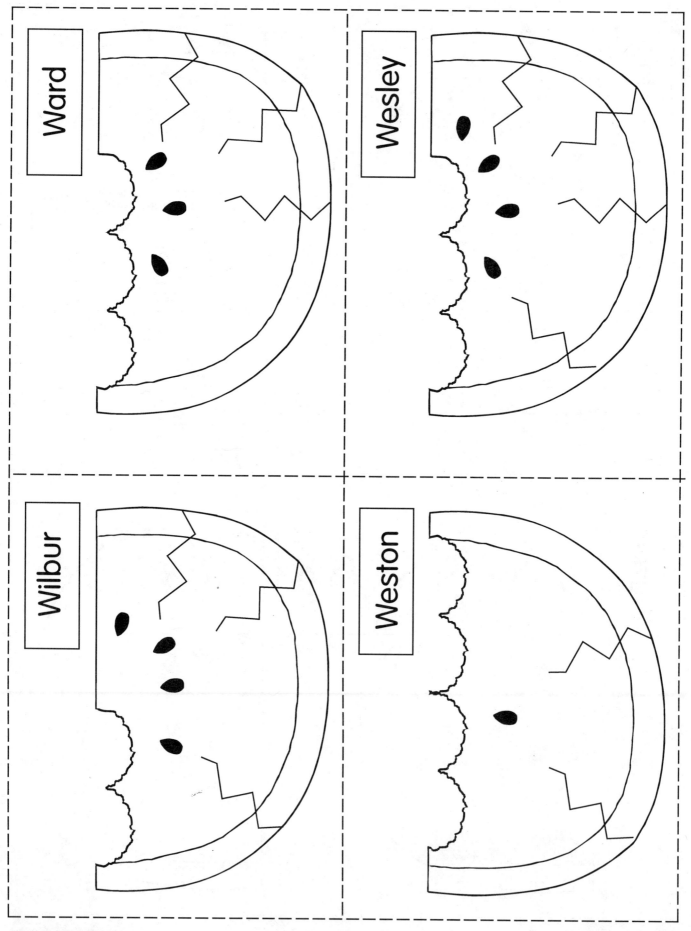

Ward

Wesley

Wilbur

Weston

Hand-On Thinking Activities

Note: Reproduce this sign to place on the table to identify each center.

fold

Mouth-watering Watermelons

Thinking Skills - *interpreting, organizing*
Number of students at this center - *up to 4*
Time required at center - *25 minutes*

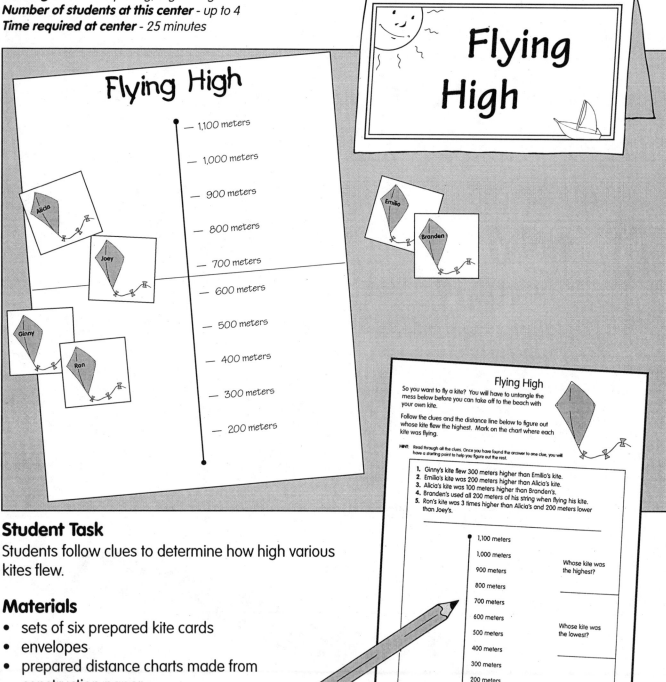

Student Task

Students follow clues to determine how high various kites flew.

Materials

- sets of six prepared kite cards
- envelopes
- prepared distance charts made from construction paper
- student record sheet on page 147
- center sign on page 149

Teacher Notes

1. Duplicate the kites on page 148 four times. Color, cut out and laminate the cards. Put each set in an envelope.

2. Prepare distance charts for students at this center. Glue two pieces of 12" X 18" (30.5 x 45.7cm) construction paper. Draw a thick line down the center of the paper. Make a mark every 2 inches (5 cm). Label as shown.

3. Review with students how to solve this type of thinking problem before they begin the center.

Flying High

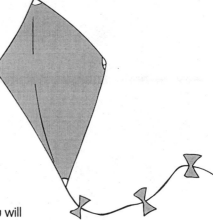

So you want to fly a kite? You will have to untangle the mess below before you can take off to the beach with your own kite.

Follow the clues and the distance line below to figure out whose kite flew the highest. Mark on the chart where each kite was flying.

HINT: Read through all the clues. Once you have found the answer to one clue, you will have a starting point to help you figure out the rest.

1. Ginny's kite flew 300 meters higher than Emilio's kite.
2. Emilio's kite was 200 meters higher than Alicia's kite.
3. Alicia's kite was 100 meters higher than Branden's.
4. Branden's used all 200 meters of his string when flying his kite.
5. Ron's kite was 3 times higher than Alicia's and 200 meters lower than Joey's.

1,100 meters

1,000 meters

900 meters

800 meters

700 meters

600 meters

500 meters

400 meters

300 meters

200 meters

0

Whose kite was the highest?

_____

Whose kite was the lowest?

_____

Hand-On Thinking Activities

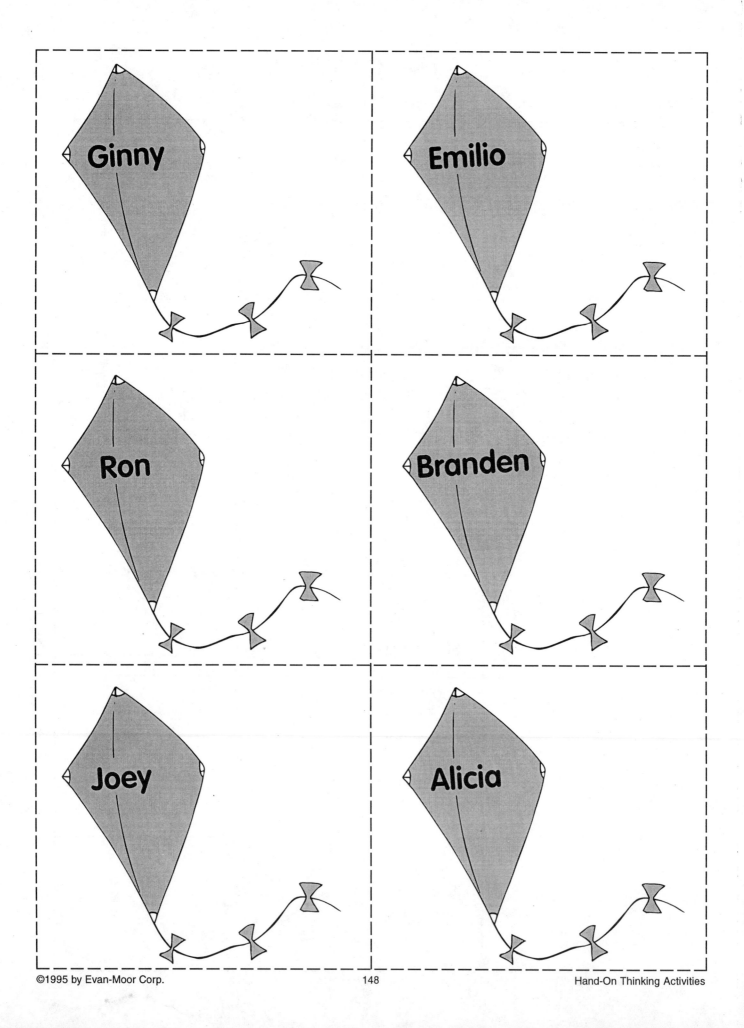

Hand-On Thinking Activities

Note: Reproduce this sign to place on the table to identify each center.

fold

Hand-On Thinking Activities

Thinking Skill - *following directions*
Number of students at this center - *2 or 4*
Time required at center - *25 minutes*

Student Task

Students create a container in which they will make ice cream following a recipe.

Materials

For each group of 2 students:

> 6 ounces (177 ml) of evaporated milk
> 3 cups (250 ml) of whole milk
> 1/2 cup (120 ml) sugar
> 1 egg
> 1/2 teaspoon (2.5 ml) vanilla extract
> ice cubes
> rock salt

Generial materials:

- small coffee cans with tight fitting plastic lids
- large coffee cans with tight fitting plastic lids
- wide masking tape
- large bucket of water for rinsing cans between each group
- student record sheet on page 151
- center sign on page 152

Teacher Notes

1. A volunteer would be helpful in this center.

2. Students work in teams of two, mixing and making the ice cream following the directions on their record sheets.

3. Have the parent volunteer accompany the students outside when they are ready to roll the cans. Ice water tends to leak even though the lids are taped.

Frozen Fun

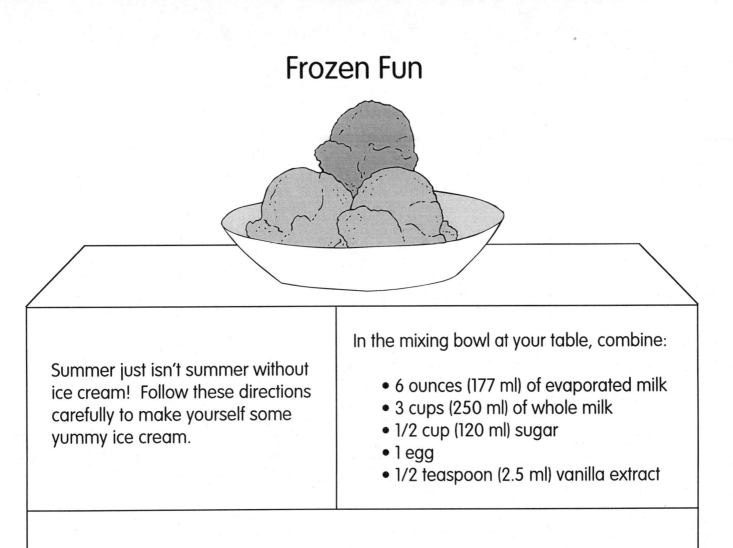

Summer just isn't summer without ice cream! Follow these directions carefully to make yourself some yummy ice cream.

In the mixing bowl at your table, combine:

- 6 ounces (177 ml) of evaporated milk
- 3 cups (250 ml) of whole milk
- 1/2 cup (120 ml) sugar
- 1 egg
- 1/2 teaspoon (2.5 ml) vanilla extract

1. Mix all of the ingredients together thoroughly. Make sure the sugar is completely dissolved.

2. Pour the mixture into a small coffee can. Place the plastic lid tightly on the can. Put a strip of masking tape around the lid, sealing it to the can.

3. Place the small can into your large, empty coffee can. Layer rock salt and ice around the smaller can, all the way to the top. Place the lid on the large can. Seal it with masking tape just as you did the smaller can.

4. Roll the can back and forth to your partner for seven minutes. Remove the lids, stir the ice cream, making sure to scrape the sides. Put the lid back on the small can and retape it. Add more rock salt and ice. Put the lid back on the large can. Roll it for another seven minutes. Check the ice cream for hardness.

5. Scoop out the ice cream into two bowls. One student will do the scooping and serving, and the partner will get to pick the bowl he or she wants first!

 Hand-On Thinking Activities

Note: Reproduce this sign to place on the table to identify each center.

fold

Thinking Skills - interpreting, designing, organizing
Number of students at this center - up to 4
Time required at center - 25 minutes

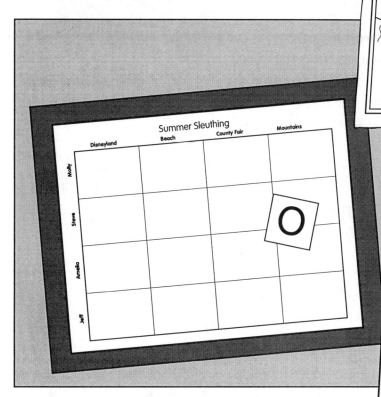

Summer Sleuthing

Summer Sleuthing
Part One

Jeff, Amelia, Steve, and Molly are lucky enough to go on vacations this summer. One went to Disneyland, another went to the beach, a third went to the county fair, and the fourth went to the mountains. Following the clues below, decide where each child went. Use the X and O cards to help you solve the mystery. Record your findings on the grid below. Good Luck!

1. Jeff is allergic to salt.

2. Steve belongs to the 4-H Club and has entered his cow in a competition in his capital city.

3. Amelia loves the smell of trees and will get a lot of chances to do so on her vacation.

• Put an **X** in the box when a child does not visit a vacation area.

• Put an **O** in the box when you know for sure a child does go to a vacation area.

Student Task

Students use a grid to help them follow a list of clues to determine where four children went on vacation.

Materials

- prepared grid mats
- **X** and **O** cards on page 74
- student record sheet on pages 154 and 155
- center sign on page 157

Teacher Notes

1. You will need to prepare the following materials for each student at the center:
   grid mat - page 156
   envelope containing **X** and **O** cards - page 74
   copies of student record sheets - pages 154 and 155
   Cut out the grids, adhere them to 8" x 12" (20.5 X 30.5 cm) construction paper, and label them as shown.

2. Students will use the cards to try and solve the puzzle. It is important that they follow the directions carefully. They need to place the **X** cards in squares when a child did NOT go on a vacation and an **O** card if the child DID go on a vacation. For example:

   If a child went to the beach, an **O** is placed in the box. **X** cards are placed in the other boxes after that child's name on the grid. By following this procedure, the student will end up with one **O** in each row marking the vacation spot the child visited.

Summer Sleuthing
Part One

Jeff, Amelia, Steve, and Molly are lucky enough to go on vacations this summer. One went to Disneyland, another went to the beach, a third went to the county fair, and the fourth went to the mountains. Following the clues below, decide where each child went. Use the X and O cards to help you solve the mystery. Record your findings on the grid below. Good luck!

---

1. Jeff is allergic to salt.

2. Steve belongs to the 4-H Club and has entered his cow in a competition in his capital city.

3. Amelia loves the smell of trees and will get a lot of chances to do so on her vacation.

- Put an **X** in the box when a child does not visit a vacation area.

- Put an **O** in the box when you know for sure a child does go to a vacation area.

	Disneyland	beach	county fair	mountains
Jeff				
Amelia				
Steve				
Molly				

beach:

mountains:

Disneyland:

county fair:

Who went where?

Summer Sleuthing
Part 2

Here's your chance to build a mystery for another student. Use the cards and grid to create three or four clues which will help your partner figure out who went where on their vacation. You can use the same vacation spots or create your own. Find a partner to try and solve your mystery!

- Put an X in the box when a child does not go to a vacation spot.
- Put an O in the box when you know for sure a child does go to a vacation spot.

Clue 1

_____

_____

Clue 2

_____

_____

Clue 3

_____

_____

Clue 4

_____

_____

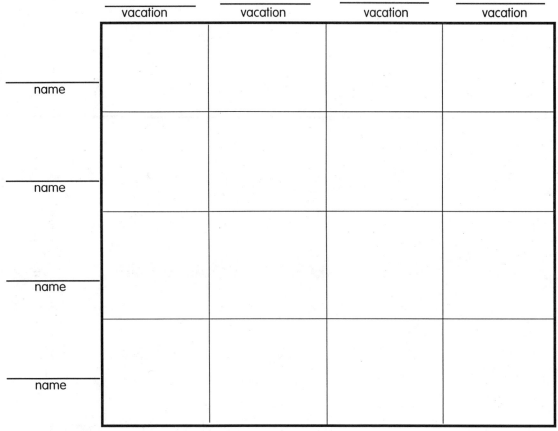

Jeff **Amelia** **Steve** **Molly**

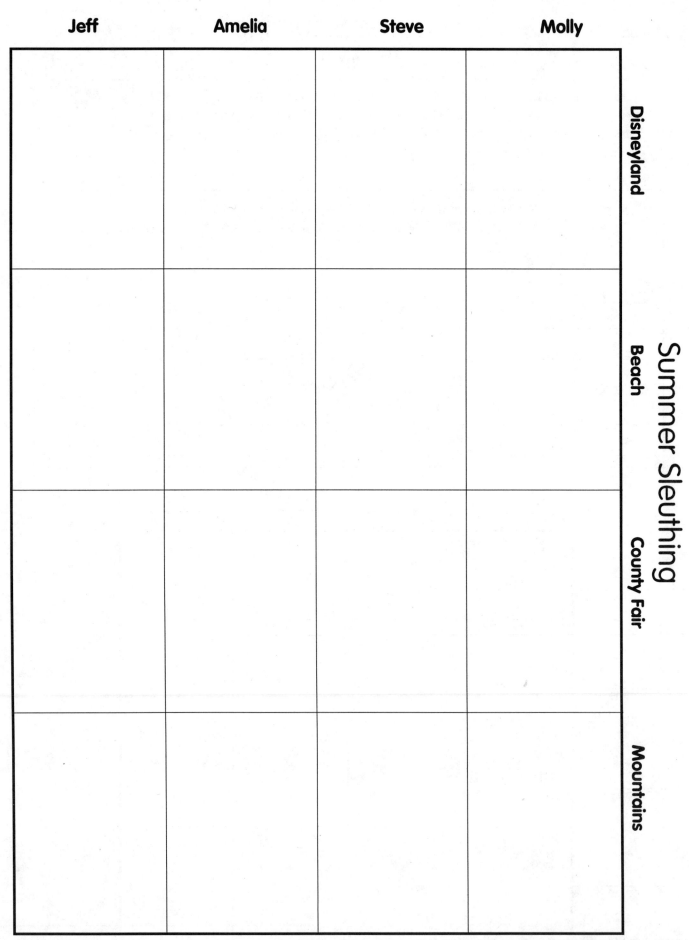

Summer Sleuthing

Disneyland

Beach

County Fair

Mountains

Hand-On Thinking Activities

Note: Reproduce this sign to place on the table to identify each center.

fold

 Hand-On Thinking Activities

Thinking Skills - *estimating, interpreting*
Number of students at this center - *up to 4*
Time required at center - *25 minutes*

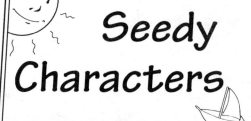

Seedy Characters

Wurk with your partner to count the seeds in these fruits and vegetables. Take one sample at a time and count the seeds. Record your findings on the chart below.

- If you have a whole fruit or vegetable record the number of seeds you counted.
- If you only have 1/2 a fruit or vegetable, multiply your findings by 2.
- 1/4 of a fruit or vegetable, multiply your

Fruit or Vegetable	Size of piece: whole, 1/2, 1/4	Number of seeds	Times 2 or 4?	Total seeds for a whole fruit

Which fruit or vegetable contained the most seeds? _____

Which contained the fewest? _____

Why do you think some fruits and vegetables have so many seeds and others have so few?

_____

_____

Student Task

Students estimate the number of seeds a piece of fruit or vegetable will contain. They then research to see how close they were to their estimate.

Materials

- provide a selection of fresh fruits and vegetables containing easy-to count seeds
- a platter
- toothpicks for removing seeds
- paper towels
- a paper plate for each student
- Handi-wipes for cleaning hands
- trash can to dispose of waste
- student record sheet on page 159
- center sign on page 160

Teacher Notes

1. Students should work in pairs to reduce volume of produce needed.

2. Leave some fruits or vegetables whole. Cut others into halves or quarters.

3. Students may eat the samples when they are finished.

Seedy Characters

Work with your partner to count the seeds in these fruits and vegetables. Take one sample at a time and count the seeds. Record your findings on the chart below.

- If you have a whole fruit or vegetable record the number of seeds you counted.
- If you have only 1/2 a fruit or vegetable, multiply your findings by 2.
- If you have only 1/4 of a fruit or vegetable, multiply your findings by 4.

Fruit or Vegetable	Size of piece: whole, 1/2, 1/4	Number of seeds	Times 2 or 4?	Total seeds for a whole fruit

Which fruit or vegetable contained the most seeds? _____

Which contained the fewest? _____

Why do you think some fruits and vegetables have so many seeds and others have so few?

_____

_____

Note: Reproduce this sign to place on the table to identify each center.

fold

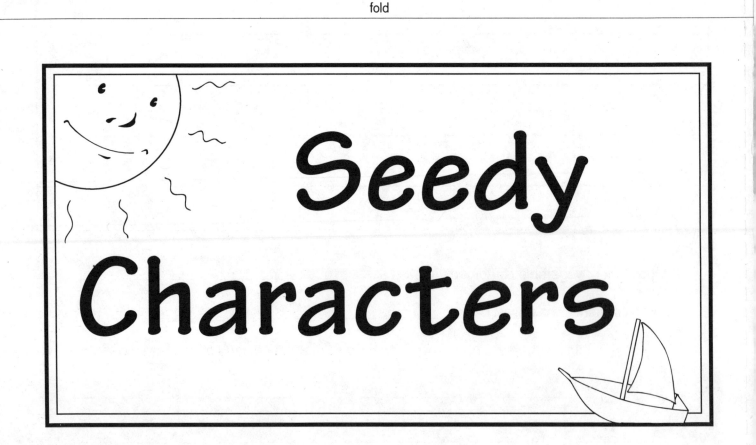

Seedy Characters